Mary Alice Seymour

Life and Letters of Louis Moreau Gottschalk

Mary Alice Seymour

Life and Letters of Louis Moreau Gottschalk

ISBN/EAN: 9783743345003

Manufactured in Europe, USA, Canada, Australia, Japa

Cover: Foto ©ninafisch / pixelio.de

Manufactured and distributed by brebook publishing software (www.brebook.com)

Mary Alice Seymour

Life and Letters of Louis Moreau Gottschalk

LIFE AND LETTERS

OF

LOUIS MOREAU GOTTSCHALK.

By OCTAVIA HENSEL,

HIS FRIEND AND PUPIL.

"Nor blame I Death, because he bare
  The use of virtue out of earth:
  I know transplanted human worth
Will bloom and profit otherwhere.
    .   .   .   .
"A life that all the muses decked
  With gifts of grace that might express
  All-comprehensive tenderness,
All subtilizing intellect."
                    TENNYSON.

BOSTON:
OLIVER DITSON AND COMPANY,
277 WASHINGTON STREET.
NEW YORK: C. H. DITSON & CO.
1870.

Entered, according to Act of Congress, in the year 1870,
BY OLIVER DITSON & CO.,
In the Office of the Librarian of Congress, at Washington.

STEREOTYPED BY C. J. PETERS & SON,
5 WASHINGTON ST., BOSTON.

I CANNOT give these pages to the public before thanking those who have so kindly encouraged me in this my tribute of love and admiration.

First, to my dear friends,

CELESTINE AND CLARA GOTTSCHALK,

am I most grateful for aiding me with reminiscences of their brother, and the kind and cordial sympathy they express in my work.

To Mr. FRANCIS G. HILL, Mr. GRENVILLE D. WILSON, and Col. CHICKERING, of Boston;

To Mrs. CLARA M. BRINKERHOFF, Mr. GEORGE WILLIAM WARREN, Mr. RICHARD HOFFMANN, and Messrs. HALL & SONS, of New York;

To Mr. CHARLES VEZIN and Miss ANNIE MEYERS, of Philadelphia;

To Mr. GEORGE P. UPTON of Chicago, —

am I indebted for encouragement and aid. From the laurel leaves their hands have brought, I have twined a wreath with the simple love and gratitude which my heart held, and must ever hold, for my dear master and friend, LOUIS MOREAU GOTTSCHALK.

OCTAVIA HENSEL.

BOSTON, August, 1870.

have loved him, their heart's treasure; and they thank you, from their hearts, for trying to give the world an idea of what they once had the happiness to possess, and now have lost!

He has been — our darling Moreau — every thing to us, ever since I can remember, — loving, affectionate, yet firm. As we were separated from father, whose calling kept him in New Orleans, Moreau was looked up to with reverence; and in all our childish troubles and joys we went to him (even in preference to our dearest mother), sure to find there sympathy.

He took especial delight in my progress in music, because he thought I would play well one day: and he would often call me, when he had friends, to ask me to play; which I did on one piano, while he at the other was playing most elaborate harmonies and variations to my simple melody, immensely enjoying the fact that *I thought it was I who was playing the whole!*

My sister Celestine, who is older than myself, has written what she remembers of him when they were children together. Had you not been so pressed for time, I would have sent you some extracts of his letters when a little boy; but I do not like to keep you waiting.

We intend going to New York for a short time. The remains of our beloved lost one will be brought from Rio; and we shall be there to gaze for the last time on his darling loved face, and pay him the last tribute of love and respect.

You tell me that he was kind to you. I am not surprised at it, but would have wondered if it had been otherwise. *He could no more help being generous and loving* than he could help having been invested with the genius given him of God! We have had no other support than him *for years.* He sent us regularly forty pounds a month, besides giving us all the money from his music published in Europe; and he would say constantly, "Dearest sisters, have you enough money to be comfortable? If not, tell me, and I will send more."

Last Christmas, twelvemonth, he wrote such a loving letter! (This Christmas he did not write: if he did, they destroyed it.) "Think," said he, "how blessed we are to love each other as we do! Think of the happiness of meeting again, strong in each other's love."

I think my sister has not told you our names. We are four sisters, and one brother. *Celestine* is the eldest; I, *Clara;* *Augusta* and *Blanche*. *Gaston* is our brother's name. Poor dear Edward was between Celestine and me. We were educated in Paris.

. . . .

I must close for post. With very kind regards from my sisters and myself,
  I remain, dear madam,
    Yours sincerely,
      CLARA GOTTSCHALK.

PREFACE.

"You know I don't care for tuberoses and jasmines. . . . I have enough of the tropics in my nature; . . . but send me blue violets and heliotrope: they soothe me into better thoughts, and make me more worthy to be

"Your sincere friend,

"L. M. Gottschalk."

Violets and heliotrope he ever asked of one to whom he wrote those words. The flowers themselves shall be placed upon his grave; but, in the spirit of their symbolism, I offer to his memory these words and thoughts, caught from the sunlight of his genius, nourished by remembrance of his kindly words and kindlier deeds.

ADAGIO.

"Take me, oh! take me, while my life is glory.
    Ere I be weary, take me to thy rest;
Ere love be feeble, or my locks be hoary:
    E'en in my beauty take me to be blest.

. . . .

Young is my spirit, crowned with dewy roses;
    Fresh is my life, as lilies freshly blown.
Love for its sweetness and its hope reposes
    On Thee, Eternal, on Thy smile alone."

. . . .

"What he suffered bodily was transmuted into a suffering of the soul. Who is there that can measure this action and re-action of body and soul?"

"Who inherit, instead of motive powers,
Impulsions God supplied;
Instead of vital spirit,
A clear informing beauty;
Instead of creature duty,
Submission calm as rest."

LOUIS MOREAU GOTTSCHALK.

"Sonata quasi una Fantasia."

PIANISSIMO.

BEETHOVEN'S "Moonlight Sonata," full of life's saddest yet richest experience, preluded by *adagio* of passionate longing over love too pure for earth denied, aptly symbolizes the character and life of one whose sweet spirit and noble soul has now finished its work in this world.

As *artistes* rarely interpret Beethoven alike; so dissimilar natures who glance over these sketches may find in them nothing but rhythmic measures, phrases of poetic beauty, but made up contrary to received methods of biographical memoirs: others may feel their truth, and learn from them to rightly estimate a life full of poetic beauty, earnestness, and unsatisfied longings after all that is highest and noblest in human existence.

"The Moonlight Sonata" has been chosen as guide in interpreting the life of Louis Moreau Gottschalk, as it stands among the works of Beethoven alone, or rather contrary, in the arrangement of its movements, to other sonatas. As the *adagio* is first given; so the calm and peaceful childhood of the boy was passed in the tropical beauty of a Southern clime. Surrounded by love, guided by the tenderness of a mother's sympathy, guarded by the calm judgment and deeply-loving heart of a father, the child gathered into his soul tones of passionate love, and trust in human sympathy. The exquisite luxuriance of Nature, the perfumes of the tropics, steeped his every sense in ecstasies of sensuous delight; and the murmuring of the breeze among the rosy-silver magnolia-blooms, the golden haze of moonlight flung through orange-groves, the crimson hue of camellia and scarlet pomegranate, wove before his baby vision a picture of delight and restful joy never afterwards effaced. True, it did not fully solace and still the longings of a soul far reaching into the depths of infinite love: but it filled his whole being with a fervor and worship of the beautiful, that never found free utterance save when it received assurances of the approach of a kindred spirit; and then the long-treasured dreams would unfold themselves, and through woof and warp of exquisite texture would glitter the pure pearls of truth, the diamond-flash of intellect, and the amethystine splendor of a sorrow too deep for human sympathy.

And perhaps here it would be well to quote the criticism of one whose charming appreciation of music is only exceeded by the culture of her style in expressing her thoughts : — *

. . . "Gottschalk's music is not so Hebraic as tropical; it suggests present and keen pleasures; it is too warm; and, like all the sweets and enjoyments of that region which gave birth to his genius, it is apt to pall. Even the sweet, luscious 'Ricordati' overwhelms one with its exuberant, fond, sensual melody: it is not pure enough for the stately pomegranates and bells of the synagogues. Mendelssohn is alone Hebraic. Both composers have rich, warm coloring, expressions of exquisite sentimentality; but in one it is a present, vivid enjoyment, in the other a deep, melodious echo of a solemn poetical past. In Mendelssohn, 'Le passé y joue un plus grand rôle que le présent : qui dit passé dit poésie ; le passé n'est il pas la jeunesse de notre imagination ?'"

. . . .

It is just and true ; but, had she known Gottschalk personally, I feel that she would have found in his compositions, not so much the music of present joy as the remembrance of past delights,

* Anna H. M. Brewster: "Compensation."

ity, but guarded well the key that gave admittance to his own true heart.

Dissimulation he never fully learned: therefore the armor he wore, of quiet hauteur and nonchalance, received the sneers of those who did not know him. Alas, poor world! judging as it does from appearances, how terribly it is often deceived! If the heaven of St. John's Apocalypse has no foundation save in the brilliant imagination of that loving disciple, it at least holds this one truth, that "there shall in no wise enter into it any thing that defileth, neither whatsoever worketh abomination or maketh a lie."

We know that preludes of sorrow and sadness thrill before every heart-beat of earthly joy: but, in the glorious hereafter, a God of love "shall wipe away all tears;" and "there shall be no more death, neither sorrow nor crying, neither shall there be any more pain; for the former things are passed away."

PIANO, DECRESCENDO.

> "You thought my heart too far diseased;
> You wonder, when my fancies play,
> To find me gay among the gay,
> Like one with any trifle pleased." — TENNYSON.

"POR la calle de despues, se va a la casa de nunca," murmured Moreau Gottschalk as he arose from the piano, and handed the duo "William Tell" to his pupil. "Who walks in the streets of *by and by* will stop in the house of *never*," he repeated in English. "Now, little hand, write that proverb on your music here, and remember me; and so, 'good-by.'" He raised the hand to his lips, and turned from the room.

"I will write those words in my memory, Mr. Gottschalk, and never say 'by and by' again. Before you return, I will learn every thing you ever wrote, and without my notes too." The young girl caught a pencil from the hand of her governess, who stood beside the piano, and motioned to Gottschalk to write the Spanish proverb.

"*C'est possible*," he replied, as he wrote the words he had spoken, "I may never return; but don't look so grave: listen to this good-by I will play for you."

He reseated himself at the piano: a few *minore* arpeggios rippled over the ivory keys, then flashed out a *motivo* so wild, so joyous, that the sorrow of parting was forgotten, and the magnetic flash of hope and joy, born amid the mysteries of harmony, thrilled the listener's heart. "Yes, that is all *you, your very self*. No one but Moreau Gottschalk could describe his own heart so exactly. You cannot keep to the *minore*."

"I don't wish to do so," he replied simply. "But this is a good-by for you alone. Tell me what it says."

A simple chorale, grand in minor chords, gave the theme; and then a slumber-song, weird and wild, wound amid the mazes of the *motivo* carried by the bass. Fainter and stiller grew the melody, until it was hushed in a *minore* so thrillingly pathetic, that death could bring no more intense sorrow to friendly hearts. And so he said "Good-by," and left his young pupil bitterly weeping.

The following morning, a note written on delicately rose-tinted paper came to her: —

"Are you not now convinced that I *can* keep to the *minore?* There is more *minore* in my heart than the world gives me credit for. Who cares? I choose to live *allegro:* death's *andante* shall never find the *presto* of my life's *sonata* unfinished.

. . . "If I never see you again, remember only

LEGATO.

> "His heart was like the ocean:
> It had storm and ebb and flow;
> And many a pearl was hidden
> In its silent depths below." — HEINE.

HIS character showed great inconsistencies. Impulse ruled rather than guided him. Some one has remarked of a similar nature, "His imagination controlled him more than his reason, and, being less firm, let the folds fly loose; and so his character showed its inconsistencies."

Euphorion in Goethe's drama, the child of Faust and Helen, that strange union of luxuriance and deep reasoning power, passionate longing and calm self-control, might better express his faults and virtues than any words his friends can use. He was a wayward, passionate child, but noble and generous in his impulses, led by a glance or a word against his better judgment, but sorely repenting his follies when brought back to himself by a gentler yet firmer nature than his own; promising to act more wisely, ever repeating that "errors repented of have no past," but forgetting that "their future must be one of atonement and amendment."

Of a delicate, nervous organization, his physical strength depended much on the state of his feelings; and, when excited by society, he gave back the kind of pleasure he received. Truly musician-like, he kept to the tone that happened to be given by those around him. If, among his gay and thoughtless companions, he was ready for frolic and mirth, careless of consequences, the next hour would find him calmly, quietly seated in a friend's parlor, absorbed in some poem, or arranging a bouquet of freshly-cut flowers, and talking as only a true lover of Nature can talk of the sentiments they inspire. At such times, his life-theme seemed only a gentle preluding, full of complex harmonies too intricate to be easily apprehended by the careless observer; but to one whose sympathies were quickened by the magnetic power of his voice-tone, and the veiled spiritual expression of his eyes, the themes were no longer intricate, but they were mere *voluntaries*, that might have widened into glorious symphonies worthy the intellect of a Beethoven.

His nature was full of religious sentiment: music wove about him a realm of waking dreams, an approach to the infinite, which words could never express. No sight, no sound, in Nature can unfold the mysterious depths of a human soul, which has power in itself to form out of the chaos of sound an all-encompassing realm, into which, through tension of thought and observation, we can penetrate, and find that chaos no longer " without form, and void."

It is only a musician who can describe or understand a nature like Gottschalk's: he was far beyond the reach of common human sympathies. His powers of adaptation were wonderful, — too good for his own benefit; for careless observers saw in him nothing but " a musical dandy," and said, " He is no true artist, merely a musical bonbon for sentimental ladies." They are right as far as they go; but he was something more to those friends who had intellect enough to demand true art and intellect from him. Unfortunately, they formed but a small portion of the society in which he was obliged to mingle at the North.

His faults were merely mistakes, — the result of his generous, passionate nature, and a pliability of head and heart that seemed a constitutional defect. " Spoiled by too much flattery in his younger life," say some who strive to exculpate him. It has been wisely said, " Great natures are never injured by appreciation and preference, even when frankly and openly expressed: they are encouraged by it, and grow nobler; nor do they ever misunderstand it. It is only the petty, inferior mind which puts a wrong construction on such regard, and wounds us by its vanity and conceit." Moreau Gottschalk was not spoiled by flattery. His mind was neither petty nor inferior, nor was he vain or conceited in the presence of true merit. In the presence of those who boasted rather loudly, he may have arrogated to himself more scientific knowledge than he possessed, — a very common fault in *artistes* of both sexes.

Deeper, more grievous faults may have been his; but, God be thanked! his most intimate friends never saw them, never knew he possessed them. Has not " Oüida " somewhere said, " Scandals are like dandelion seeds: they are arrow-headed, stick where they fall, and bring forth and multiply fourfold. Scandals and dandelions, both weeds, relished by donkeys " ? A truth too obvious to be commented upon here.

It has been regretted by many, that Gottschalk allowed himself to make a trade, as it were, of his genius, and descend to flatter public taste, rather than aid in raising the standard of music in this country. He knew himself too well to take a position his impulsive nature would never allow him to hold. He preferred to allure, rather than to be an authority. He inspired in every audience musical appreciation, and guided them gradually to more strict musical apprehension; then he stepped aside, and left the field of scientific and classical lore to older, steadier heads than his own. He never sought to reform, to revolutionize: he knew he could not be a leader of the classic school; but he did glorious picket-duty, rode many a raid right gallantly, and brought many a heart captive into the royal realm of Music.

Industry formed little part of his nature; and yet he could be an earnest, untiring student when the necessity was put upon him. The concert-room was the last place to fully understand his wonderful talent, — a talent upheld by genius and sentiment. The music he played in public blinds one who would study his true character. It seems the foam on the top of his goblet of life. Once or twice is that froth flung aside, and his nobler nature speaks to us in the "Marche Solennelle," and the *motivo* of the "Marche de Nuit." Again, in the "Ricordati," "Berceuse," and the *majeure* of "Serenade," his heart speaks in simplest strains. But his "Souvenir de la Havane," "Bamboula," "Bananier," "Ojos Criollos," are mere shams for the concert-room; and no one more thoroughly laughed at them than their author. "It is only mediocrity that pays," he often repeated; "and, as I must live, I must be willing to please others, even if not myself."

To rightly apprehend Gottschalk's talent, it was necessary to hear him alone, or with two or three chosen friends. He would seat himself at the piano, — always more readily if a vase of his favorite violets and heliotrope stood near, — and the improvisations that flowed beneath his skilful fingers came from his happy, loving heart, as breezes through an orange-grove.

At times his heart was silent; and then the brain wove its intricate harmonies into combinations so fantastic, so weird and wildly sweet, that they seemed like seraph voices chanting from the far-off spheres in stillness of midnight; and then a rapid modulation amid arpeggios and chromatics would flash out as the clear cold northern lights in a wintry sky: these fading, the heart asserted its sway; and melodies languishing in dreamy reverie of sunnier lands, amid perfumes of magnolia and orange groves, thrilled with passionate longing the loving soul that listened. Again, when the *maestro's* heart and mind strove with each other for mastery, a simple theme would for a moment plunge the hearer into a Lethean stream, so near the fountain of tears that the poor heart would tremble in a suspense exquisitely painful. Emerging from the momentary forgetfulness, sad, slow, minor strains would call up the purer, better nature; and tears such as little children shed over their lost or broken treasures would suffuse the eyes: but, like the sorrows of little children, these soon passed; for the April sunshine of his heart streamed over the tear-laden *motivo*, and it broke into trilling of birds, and the golden sunlight of simple melodies. In such an hour, "Home, Sweet Home" flashed along the keys, and became a home of happiness glowing in the holiest love. Rising from the piano, he would glance around the group, give one long look into the eyes of the one nearest to him in sympathy, and, with a weary smile, sink into his favorite fauteuil, and remain silent for hours. On one of these occasions, a little child approached him with an orange, and said, "It's all I *dot:* but, when you play, I *hear* the angels sing which mamma tells me *'bout;* so I *div* it all to you." Gottschalk lifted the beautiful boy in his arms, and, laying his head close to the golden ringlets of the child, whispered, "Tell me about the angels. I haven't any mamma now to tell me."

Who can know all that passed between the two, as they nestled close to each other by the fireside, — the short, dark curls of the man mingling with the sunny ringlets of the child, whose sweet voice lisped the wondrous story of the "In excelsis gloria." "Come, little one, and tell me more pretty stories," was his greeting ever afterwards. God grant, that, with that angel-child, he now hears the glorious harmony of the seraph voices that sometimes glanced into his earthly dreams!

CRESCENDO.

"Now flashing, sharp on sharp, along,
Exultant in a mounting throng;
Now dying off into a song

Fed upon minors, — starry sounds
Moved on free-paced, in silver rounds,
Enlarging liberty with bounds.

And every rhythm that seemed to close
Survived in confluent under-flows,
Symphonious with the next that rose."
MRS. BROWNING.

WHEN Herz entered the concert-rooms of America, and aroused the dormant musical apprehension of the audiences who crowded to hear his brilliantly rapid variations on well-known melodies, a new impulse was given to piano-music; and opera fantasias, but mostly quadrilles and waltzes, were heard on every side.

Then came Maurice Strakosch, with his bravouras and polkas surcharged with octaves and chromatic passages, *con fuoco, con brio;* and hardly had the echo of his *galops* died away, when the quiet, coldly intellectual Thalberg spread before us the frozen rainbows of his icy intellect. The smooth harmony, woven in web and woof with genius and scientific toil, well repaid the earnestly intellectual lover of music, and refreshingly cooled, while it dazzled with prismatic light, the over-wrought brain. Exquisite finish, faultless mechanism, harmony pure as perfect, — Thalberg gave us statues of marble, in music poems.

As this radiant iceberg floated nearer and nearer the shores of our life-ocean, chilling yet charming our hearts, a warm breeze from tropical groves of magnolia and orange flung its delicious languor upon our senses, and warmed our hearts into magnetic *rapport* with its passionate luxuriance.

Louis Moreau Gottschalk stood before us, and captivated our senses by speaking to our hearts. No *con fuoco, con brio, tranquillo, morendo*, cheered, pleased, and quieted us; but *scintillante, animato, brilliante, rapido*, awoke us to consciousness of heart-life. The "Danse Ossianique" glittered with diamonds, not of ice and snow, but *brilliantes* like those found in the beds of rivers which wander through the luxuriance of tropical vegetation. When the majestic measures of the "Grande Marche Solennelle" and "Marche de Nuit" prepared the way for the *religioso* of the "Last Hope," again our hearts warmed to him whose pure friendship could utter such *prière du soir* for one whose mourning, motherly heart asked of him " *une petite mélodie* ULTIMA ESPERANZA!"

What if the "Jota Aragonese" recalled the gay dances of the sunny South, and the "Banjo" described an unintellectual throng of black faces and curly wool, or "La Gallina" caused even little children to say, "Oh, hear the chickens pick up corn!" what if he took us into human life and mirth: are we debasing art by asserting our humanity? It is a stupid fancy ball, where every one has the dress and dignity of royalty; and shall we, in this great fancy-ball world, sacrifice our natural tastes by striving to attune our minds to the concert-pitch of a purely intellectual dictator?

Louis Moreau Gottschalk was no imitator; he never sought after mere effects; he listened to the murmuring of the breeze among the pines of our Northern forests, and "Murmurs Æolians" breathed themselves into life. If the "Reflets du Passe" or "The Dying Poet" saddened for a moment his joyous heart, then "The Dove" came on its errand of peace. When "Pastorella e Cavalliere" told its simple story, old men smiled, and maidens' eyes filled with mischievous mirth. Doubtless these grave old gentlemen would have appeared more imposing, had they paid studious attention to the prompting of intellectually classic critics, and frowned at such human nonsense; while maidens would have appeared more strong-minded, and intellectually virtuous, to have sung

"Elijah," and ruined their voices in attempting Beethoven's "Leonora." But human nature asserted itself; and Moreau Gottschalk, with his sunny smile, and generous, loving heart, won them forever by his beautiful, trustful reliance in Nature and Truth.

God be thanked, Moreau Gottschalk was not afraid to show his humanity, and establish a school, a music, of his own. As Teniers in Antwerp led in the van of the Belgic school of art, as Turner in England, as Poussin and Lorraine, have given their impress to the naturalness of the French school; so in America, Moreau Gottschalk stands at the head of the noble army of — yes, martyrs, *artists who dare to be themselves*, and abhor the dilettanteism and affectation of self-reliant musical critics. He has done more for the advancement of piano-music than any man of this century. He is not as the pianist of the past, he may not be the pianist of the future; but he is the pianist of the present. Criticism may array itself against him; criticism loves a bright and shining mark: but criticism never stifled Chopin, nor can it peril the fame of Gottschalk. Unlike, yet "like in difference," alone they stand, Chopin and Gottschalk, unappreciated, never understood, save by those who were admitted into the sanctuary of their friendship; but the day is dawning, when, in spite of critics and time-honored fables, the works of Chopin and Gottschalk will be properly translated, and we will no longer stumble blindly into correct rendition of tones which from them thrilled with soul-power.

ALLEGRETTO.

"All my life long,
I have beheld with most respect the man
Who knew himself, and knew the ways before him,
And from amongst them chose considerately,
With a clear foresight, not a blindfold courage;
And, having chosen, with a steadfast mind
Pursued his purposes."

. . . .

"That man is not the most in tribulation, who, resolute of mind, walks his own way, with answerable skill to plant his steps." — TAYLOR'S PHILIP VAN ARTEVELDE.

"No one need pride himself upon genius, for it is the free gift of God; but of honest industry, and true devotion to his destiny, any man may well be proud. Indeed, this thorough integrity of purpose is itself the divine idea in its most common form; and no really honest mind is without communion with God." — FICHTE.

"I go to prove my soul:
I see my way, as birds their trackless way:
In some time — God's good time — I shall arrive.
He guides me and the bird." — BROWNING.

PIANO.

> "What wert thou then? A child most infantine,
>   Yet wandering far beyond that innocent age
> In all but its sweet looks and mien divine;
>   Even then, methought, with the world's tyrant rage
>   A patient warfare thy young heart did wage,
> When those soft eyes of scarcely conscious thought
>   Some tale, or thine own fancies, would engage
> To overflow with tears, or converse fraught
> With passion o'er their depths its fleeting light had wrought."
>
> SHELLEY.

AS the allegretto of "The Moonlight Sonata" opens with combined harmony of wondrous sweetness; so the unfolding life of the infant son of Edward Gottschalk and Aimée Marie de Braslé brought purest happiness and joy to the heart of his beautiful young mother: while the manly pride and love of his father showed deepest gratitude for the gift of a son so gentle, noble, and talented.

Of these parents it is needed to say but little: their life-work and tender care of the children born to them has its best witness in the beautiful devotion and love with which these children repaid their care. The following simple words, taken from a letter written by Celestine, their eldest daughter, are sufficient record: —

"Mamma's name was Aimée Marie de Braslé; papa's, Edward Gottschalk. He was born in London, studied to be a doctor in Leipsic, but gave it up at twenty-five years of age, and went to America, where, in the year 1828, he married our mother in New Orleans. She was but fifteen years old. In 1829, our darling brother Moreau was born; he was, we were always told, a very fair and delicate-looking baby, but most exquisitely pretty."

Not only exquisitely pretty, but exquisitely good, we learn from a less partial source than a sister's heart. If ever his baby-voice was lifted in fretful wail, the soft music of his young mother's slumber-song stilled in an instant the sorrow and pain, and wove into his soul loving melodies that were to thrill into beauteous expression throughout his glorious young life. Very early, too, did his tiny baby-fingers assert their life-work.

His sister tells us, "When Moreau was three years old, our mother, being ill, was taken to Pass Christian, to the seaside. One day, every one in the house was startled by a faint but most exquisite melody on the piano. The tone and touch were perfect. As no one in the house but mamma played that air, she was the first to rush into the drawing-room; and there, to her infinite surprise, she found little Moreau standing on a high stool, playing the melody she had sung to him in the morning.

"Papa was told of the event, and decided that Moreau should have a professor as soon as they returned to town. So Mr. Letellier, a French gentleman and a very good musician, was called to teach our little brother. When he was six years old, he began lessons in French with Monsieur Mauroy, and with Mr. Ely for violin. He improved rapidly, and could play very difficult pieces."

"One Sunday morning, during mass, the organist being unable to attend, Mr. Letellier from the choir saw Moreau kneeling in our pew: he hurried down stairs, took the little fellow in his arms, and carried him into the organ-loft, where he placed him before the organ, and told him to play. Mr. Letellier pulled the stops and used the pedals, but Moreau played the whole service, reading at sight. His delight was unbounded. He ran the whole way home, and, rushing into mamma's arms, tried to explain to her what had taken place; but the excitement of the music, the fatigue of his race, and the happy feeling of his childish success, so choked his utterance, that he could not speak a word, but only nestle in her arms and weep."

His love and admiration for his mother was very beautiful: his father, as are all fathers perhaps, was very strict; and Moreau was a little afraid of him, as indeed all the children were. But to his mother he used to go, as to an elder sister, for every thing. In speaking of this, his sister says, —

"It was charming to behold his admiration for mamma's beauty. She was his *confidante* and comforter in all things. To us, he was, so far as we can remember, the most kind, the most devoted, of brothers, — always ready to help us in our little wants, to play with us; in fact, he was and has always been *our life and light, our all.*"

In his eighth year, we are told of a charity concert he gave for the benefit of Mr. Miolau, a violinist from the French opera. This was the first concert he gave; and the success he obtained that night held brilliant promise for the future. When the concert was over, calmly and unassumingly the young boy received the thanks and congratulations of his friends, and went quietly home with his parents. The excitement did not keep him wakeful; and the events of the evening seemed quickly forgotten in the peacefulness of sleep, when suddenly the household was awakened by a magnificent serenade. Mr. Miolau and his friends, out of compliment to the child, were playing beneath his window.

We turn once more to his sister's reminiscences, and from them copy the following lines: —

"Almost every Sunday evening, Moreau used

to play at Mrs. Boyer's evening parties. Mrs. Boyer was at that time the first lady music-teacher in New Orleans. Moreau's genius was well appreciated there. At last, Mrs. Boyer urged papa to send our brother to Paris, where he could secure the very best instruction. At first, papa hesitated; for mamma could not make up her mind to part with any of us children, much less with her handsome eldest boy, her idol, of whom she was so proud. So years passed on, Moreau becoming more talented, more beautiful and good, every day. Mamma hoped that papa had forgotten all about sending our darling to Paris; but not so: one day he told mamma she must at once get Moreau ready; for he had decided to have him sail with his friend Capt. Rogers, on the ship 'La Taglioni.' Every thing was arranged for his departure; and in May, 1842, he bade us all farewell. It was the saddest parting we little ones had ever known."

In the month of March, he gave a farewell concert in St. Louis Hall, the largest, at that time, in New Orleans. An amusing episode occurred, which caused him great amusement whenever he recalled the evening. He was a slender, boyish figure, with a most childlike face; and the hairdresser, a stranger to whom he had gone to have his hair curled, supposed he was some young boy preparing for a child's party. So he told him all about the wonderful young pianist, and asked him if he did not wish he could go and hear little Gottschalk; then added, "Now, that's a stupid question; for surely such a mite as you are will enjoy your party: but you'll not have many to see you, for everybody in town is going to the concert."

In speaking of this, he once said, "If you could have seen the look of contemptuous pity the man gave me when I said I liked parties best, and then the look of astonishment that came into his face when I told him who I was, you would have laughed as heartily as I did."

His sister tells us, "Mother, being in delicate health, was kept in ignorance of the precise time of his departure. This parting proved a terrible shock to her. For a while her life was despaired of, so intense seemed her grief: she lived only in the hope of receiving letters from him; and she was not disappointed. When he arrived in Paris, he sent her a journal he had kept on board ship, in which he gives an admirable description of meeting an iceberg, and a graphic account of escape from the danger of shipwreck."

"He was placed at a private school in Paris, kept by Monsieur and Madame Dussert. He was just twelve years old, his birthday having occurred on the ship. He took lessons first, but for a short time only (not more than six months), from

Charles Hallé; but, his teaching being too careless, Madame Dussert changed him for the best professor in Paris, — Camille Stamaty, — who showed himself not only a skilful and careful teacher, but also a true, firm friend, which he ever remained. At the age of thirteen, he began the study of harmony with Mr. Maledan."

Through his aunt, La Comtesse de Lagrange, and his cousin, La Comtesse de Bourjolly, he was admitted into some of the best society in Paris. He was a frequent and welcome guest at the Duchesse de Narbonne's, where his playing excited the admiration of all true lovers of art; and many were the delicious *soirées musicales* given by the Duc de Salvandy, where the brilliant improvisations of his friend, the young Gottschalk, added delight to the hours.

It was about this time that he began to write some of his most exquisite compositions. His first was "Ossian," two delicately-written ballads for his mother's birthday; then "Danse des Ombres," which title he afterwards changed to "Danse Ossianique."

At the age of fifteen he was attacked with typhoid fever, and for three months was dangerously ill. During a long and tedious convalescence he composed "Bananier," "Savane," "Bamboula:" but the latter took him a long time to complete; for his physician forbade mental work, and sent him, with Madame Dussert, into the Ardennes, for rest and freedom from excitement.

When he returned to Paris, he bent every energy to excel in the study of harmony. He became the pupil, and soon the friend, of Hector Berlioz. In order that nothing might disturb his earnest study, he declined an invitation extended by Isabella, Queen of Spain, to visit the court at Madrid.

During the summer of 1846, he went on a pedestrian tour through the Vosges. His forgetfulness of such troublesome accompaniments as passports frequently caused him amusing detentions. At one time he reached a small town, where, having forgotten or mislaid his passport, he was taken into the police court. While waiting on a bench, he noticed one of the *gendarmes* reading a paper in which he saw his last piece announced, — "Les Colliers d'Or." By this means he managed to assure the *maire* of his identity, and by him was invited home to breakfast; and they became good friends ever afterwards.

Through his acquaintance with Pleyel, his concerts were most frequently given in Salle Pleyel, where he was assisted by his friends Marmontel, Le Couppey, Offenbach, Jos. Ascher, and many others. It was at this time that he was invited by Zimmermann, of the Paris Conservatoire, to become one of the judges at the *concours* of the conservatory.

During the winter of 1846-47, he gave a series of concerts with Berlioz, at the Italian opera. They were a most brilliant success.

In the spring of 1847, he was so wearied and overworked from his musical studies, that his physicians recommended a tour through Switzerland. At Geneva, and afterwards at Lausanne, he met the Grand Duchess of Russia, who was most kind to him, and presented him with a very elegant diamond-and-pearl pin. At Vevay, a small town on Lake Geneva, he gave a charity concert for the blind, with the proceeds from which part of the hospital was built which now bears his name.

Loaded with gifts, he returned to Paris in December to welcome his mother, sisters, and brothers, who had come to meet him. He remained with them for a year, working at his musical studies, and completing some of his most exquisite pieces, which he had composed during his tour in Switzerland. Among them we find the "Mancenillier," arranged for two pianos, "Chasse de jeune Henri," "Songe d'une Nuit d'Eté," and "La Moissonneuse Mazurka."

He did not devote himself so exclusively to the study of his art as to render him selfish to others. He gave many concerts, but all for charitable purposes. In a letter from his sister Clara, she mentions one of these concerts, and how painful his playing had been. She says, —

"He was very fond of us, and would play with the little ones on the floor for hours. Once, I remember, the day of a concert in Paris, he was amusing little Gaston with a top, when, in taking it up in his outstretched hand, he ran a splinter of wood in the finger, and had to play in the evening with a bleeding hand."

The concert which attracted the most public attention was the great charity-concert for the workmen of Mr. Pleyel. The buildings had been burned, and for three months the poor people had been in a starving condition. Gottschalk, hearing of it, immediately gave a monster concert for their benefit. His sister's account of it is too modestly simple to be ignored: —

"At the close of the concert, one of the oldest workmen stepped upon the platform, and, in the name of his fellow-workmen, made a little speech of thankfulness to Moreau, and presented him with a bouquet. It was such a pretty bouquet, I remember. Mamma got it, of course; for Moreau gave all his flowers to her."

In the spring of 1849, he started for a concert-tour throughout France. He was feasted, courted, and loaded with every mark of distinction. When he reached Bordeaux, he heard that his father had arrived in Paris from New Orleans: so he returned immediately to the capital. His sister writes, —

"After a few days given to supremest enjoyment of our happy re-union, they went together to Bordeaux; and thither Moreau embarked for Spain, and papa came back to us."

In Spain he was most kindly received by the queen, being provided with rooms and entertained in the palace. From the king he received two orders, — that of the diamond cross of "Isabella la Catholique," and that of the "Leon d'Holstein." The sword of honor, "El Chielanero," was also presented to him. The Duc de Montpensier was among his friends and admirers. One of his finest waltzes for two pianos was composed for a *fête* given by the Duchess. As he had but short notice of the event, he composed the work in four hours. The second piano was played by Don Carlos.

It was during this visit to the Spanish capital that an incident occurred, strikingly illustrative of his romantic love of adventure, and the generous character of his impulses.

It is thus given by a friend: —

"His concerts had produced a decided sensation; in fact, had taken the people quite by storm. The furore occasioned by his success was very general: it was such as easily to fascinate the mind of an imaginative and impressible young Spanish girl, and one such was caught by the splendid glamour. She was confined to her sick chamber, even to her bed: her friends considered her near her end. But she was enthusiastically fond of music, and the fame of this celebrated young artist had inspired her with a most passionate desire to hear him. How idle the hope! Her people were in very humble circumstances, and accordingly were not in a condition to compensate the musician for so great pains as paying her a visit, and giving a concert for her exclusive benefit, would involve. But she would take no denial: she felt that she must hear this man before she died. Could she but once be entranced by his delicious, dreamy music, she could say, 'Welcome death!'

"Her request was made known to the great pianist. To the utter astonishment of all, he at once gave orders for his piano to be conveyed to her humble abode, and he himself straightway followed it. Then, by the bedside of that dying girl, he proceeded to discourse such music as only he, perhaps, under the strange circumstances, could. He was in his element. His fair listener, it need not be said, was in hers. Nay, she was only too happy. Under the stress of the rapturous and grateful emotions inspired by this kind and gratuitous service on the part of the distinguished and beautiful stranger, the frail tabernacle containing that passionate young nature was shaken, and the enfranchised spirit had flown ere he finished his final chord."

He remained in Spain for two years, and returned to Paris in the autumn of 1852, in order to say farewell to his mother and sisters, previous to sailing for New York, where his father and brother Edward awaited him.

Notwithstanding the petitions of his friends, he refused to give a public concert before his departure: he preferred to spend all the time possible with his mother and sisters. One evening, however, he invited a few friends, and played for them as he never played in public. It was a sweet, dreamy preluding of sorrowful yet prayerful hope for the future, the entrancing harmony of the present; while the joyous, sparkling memories of his past childhood flashed through the music-dreams he wove about the loving hearts who heard him, stilling their sorrow at parting, holding them spell-bound at visions so pure of the unknown future into which he was hastening.

The silent, suffering heart of his mother beat softly as she listened; the beautiful eyes of his sisters filled and overflowed with weight of tears; love tender and true filled every heart: and, when the last vibration of a passionate minor cadence trembled into silence, gentle voices whispered "Farewell," and Louis Moreau Gottschalk was never again heard in Paris.

"We part forever now, my child," murmured the soft voice of his mother as he knelt beside her, his beautiful head resting upon her bosom, his strong young arms holding her close in a loving embrace. He was silent, save the convulsive sobs that shook his frame. Both felt that they should never again meet in this world; and, amid prayers and blessings, her lips rested on his pure young brow for the last time, — fitting chrism of holiest love, a memory to calm and hallow for all time every thought, and lead him in the hour of temptation and sorrow into nobler dreams, purer, more spiritual visions of the brighter land whither she was soon called to await her first-born darling.

CRESCENDO.

"Friendly love perfecteth mankind." — BACON.

"To have found favor in thy sight
  Will still remain
A river of thought, that full of light
  Divides the plain." — MILNES.

IT is an easy matter for the biographer of one so publicly noted as Mr. Gottschalk to turn over files of old journals, and gather from them daily notices and criticisms of concerts; but it is not so easy to trace the personal history of the artist in the gratitude his kindly reception in America caused him to feel. That he was happy and grateful for these well-earned triumphs is very true; and his earlier friends all bear testimony to the simplicity and modesty with which he received congratulations, showered upon him after his first brilliant concert at Niblo's, in New York.

How well that night is recalled! In childlike wonder, a young girl had gazed at the strange name, "GOTTSCHALK," on the posters at either side the entrance to Niblo's, as she passed through Broadway in the afternoon; and in her private journal is still kept the following notice of the distinguished stranger pianist, which she cut from the evening paper after her father had laid it aside, and settled back in his " King chair " for an after-dinner nap.

It is thus that Hector Berlioz speaks of the young *artiste*: —

"Gottschalk is one of the very small number who possess all the different elements of a consummate pianist, all the faculties which surround him with an irresistible prestige, and give him a sovereign power. He is an accomplished musician: he knows just how far fancy may be indulged in expression. He knows the limits beyond which any liberties taken with the rhythm produce only confusion and disorder; and upon these limits he never encroaches. There is an exquisite grace in his manner of phrasing sweet melodies, and throwing off light touches from the higher keys. The boldness and brilliancy and originality of his play at once dazzles and astonishes, and the infantile *naïveté* of his smiling caprices, the charming simplicity with which he renders simple things, seem to belong to another individuality, distinct from that which marks his thundering energy: thus the success of M. Gottschalk before an audience of musical cultivation is immense."

Very patiently the young girl stood while her maid adjusted the pinky bows and laces of her new opera-bonnet; and carefully she shook out the folds of a pink-satin opera-cloak, as she alighted from the carriage, and took her father's arm to enter the concert-room.

The crowd of beautiful and richly-dressed women, and the low hum of conversational excitement, the flutter of fans, the expectant glances towards the stage, — how all these flash before her as she recalls the night of Gottschalk's first concert in New York. At last the hum of voices was drowned in the burst of applause that greeted the entrance of the *artiste*. There he stood, gracefully inclining towards his audience, one hand resting on the corner of the piano, the other pressed to his breast as he repeatedly bowed in acknowledgment of his enthusiastic reception. At last he seated himself at the piano, and drew off his gloves, for a moment his delicate, slender hands were half clasped or folded together, and then they poised an instant over the keys.

A magnetic thrill flashed over the audience as lightning-like arpeggios blended harmonies so full of languor and luxuriance, that one could not recall the *motivo* rippling through the fantasia he played. She cannot recall all of the programme: she only remembers the magnetic power of the music, the dreamful beauty of his eyes, and the softly outlined melancholy in his face.

"The Home Journal" of the following day contained the best criticism, perhaps, of this concert.

"Mr. Gottschalk, the American pianist, made his *début* at Niblo's Saloon on Friday, the 11th instant. We mention the date, because we are convinced that the musical history of the country will require that it should be preserved. To say that his success was of the most unequivocal description can convey to the reader's mind no idea of the *frenzy* of enthusiasm which his performance excited. His playing is precisely of the kind which most palpably hits the popular taste. His effects are strong and powerful. He dashes at the instrument as Murat charged the enemy, and has command of its most latent possibilities. His playing has the effect of an orchestra, and the modulation of a single instrument. He is the only pianist we have yet heard who can electrify and inflame an assembly. He produces the same sort and the same degree of effect as that which oratory sometimes has in times of public commotion. This is not exaggeration, as every one will bear witness who has heard him perform; but a simple statement of facts. A sober judgment of his powers as compared with those of other eminent pianists we are not prepared to give; since it was impossible not to be carried away with the enthusiasm of the occasion. But we hope to hear him again at an early day, and to consider his performance more coolly. The feeling of the audience was well expressed by a distinguished lady who attended the concert, who remarked, ' Gottschalk has the dexterity of Jaell- the power of De Meyer, and the taste of Herz.'"

But "The Tribune" of New York was nearer the truth in its criticism than any other paper, although it eulogized him somewhat awkwardly by implying that Beethoven was well enough in his way, but it had been permitted to a citizen of our republic to get ahead of classical "old fogies." Whether this was intended as a compliment at the expense of Beethoven, or of his classical supporters in this country, must be decided by personal common sense. It will be as well perhaps to give an extract from that very excellent but conservative journal which rules the Boston musical world with a rod of iron. The criticism is just, and generous inasmuch as the writer has not " *caught the spirit of the article referred to.*"

"But 'The Tribune,' usually so sound and cautious, goes ahead of all in the extravagance of its praise, and has a theory for it: namely, that it is an age of progress, and that we must not nail our notions of perfection in piano-music down to Beethoven's 'Sonatas;' and that it may be permitted to a young man, a citizen of this great 'manifest-destiny' republic, to go beyond those 'old fogies' who are cried up as 'classical.' That is the drift of it. And the implied inference is, that Beethoven was well enough in his way, but that Gottschalk has opened a new path, &c., &c. In what? So far as we are told, in mechanism, in writing music *for the piano;* so that with its natural imperfections it may, by dint of wonderful execution, in some manner represent the breadth of a full orchestra, and ring at once through all the compass of its seven octaves. Now, Beethoven and composers of creative genius write secondarily for the piano, but primarily for art; for the expression of musical ideas and inspirations born in the mind, and not made to order from the fingers. In the respects which 'The Tribune' critic mainly looks to, Gottschalk may very naturally have got beyond Beethoven, as Thalberg and Listz have done; but in the respects which give the sonatas of Beethoven their rank in history, and their value in the souls of all true music-lovers, and which are irrespective of mere mechanical adaptation to an exhaustive employment of the instrument, it sounds a little paradoxical to hear it said that these sonatas are surpassed by a young man, an American, chiefly noted for a brilliant play, and for the composition of 'Bananiers' and 'Bamboulas.' Genius, to be sure, is of no country, is the greatest of God's gifts to man, and shall be welcome, more than welcome, whenever and under whatever form it shall approach; but we cannot accept it on *such* showing (if we have rightly caught the spirit of the article referred to).

"Wishing to do full justice in the premises, and not ignore a 'new phenomenon,' we design soon to condense for our readers a history of young Gottschalk's career, from 'The Courier des États Unis,' if we can only find its facts, separable from the superlative eulogy that swells every sentence, comparing his childhood to Mozart's, his grace and delicacy to Chopin, his virtuosity in general to that of Listz and Thalberg, &c., &c."

At the pianist's second concert, Feb. 17, 1853, his playing won if possible even more applause. The programme contained many of the *executant's* compositions, — showy, brilliant, and descriptive, well suited to a New-York audience of that period, but should not be classed with programmes of the present day, and judged severely for its lightness and display of the " modern *finger-miracle* school."

" Bamboula," " Le Savane," " Bananier," and " Carnival de Venise," were admirably rendered; but the gem of the evening was the

"Jerusalem," played with Mr. Richard Hoffman. This fantasie had been composed at the request of Her Imperial Highness, Madame la Grande Duchesse, Anne de Russie, and was played for the first time at a *fête* which this princess gave in the summer-palace of La Boissiere, in honor of their Majesties the Queen of Sardinia, Prussia, Saxony, Prince Albert of Prussia, and Russian princesses innumerable.

Its grand progression of harmonies works out a unity of thought that wraps a dreamland of Eastern splendor about those who hear it, bearing them far away among the rosy oleander blooms on the banks of the Jordan, the rippling murmurs of Brook Kedron, the glorious temple-service of the earthly type of "Jerusalem the Golden," the calm moonlight of Olivet, and the mournful desolations of the Roman Legions under the Emperor of the West.

It was after this concert that a father asked of his daughter, "Will you take lessons of Thalberg, or Gottschalk?"

"Father, how can you ask such a question? Why, of Gottschalk, most assuredly! But will he give lessons?"

The question was not decided until three years later; when, at the urgent request of his numerous friends, he consented to take pupils during the six or eight weeks of his stay in New York. So, one cold March morning in the spring of 1856, she stood before Mr. Gottschalk as his pupil.

He looked at her with an expression of polite nonchalance, then raised his eyes to an exquisite painting of St. Cecilia hanging near the piano, and a few panels of Fra Angelico's angels surrounding it.

"Do you love pictures, Mr. Gottschalk?" was her first question.

"Yes," he replied, "such gems as these. Your parents have excellent taste."

She tossed her head as much as to say, "Why shouldn't they?" But, catching an amused smile trying to assert itself in Mr. Gottschalk's face, she added, "These pictures belonged to my mother's grandfather. But we think more of the engravings he collected in Europe. Come into the library: I will show them to you." She was leading the way across the hall, when he reminded her that he must first give the music-lesson. "Oh, no!" she replied: "it can wait. Pictures are much more entertaining to us both, I fancy."

"Then mademoiselle does not care for music?"

"Indeed I do, but love it too much to endure my poor attempts. It discourages me to look at a piano."

"Then I wouldn't look at it. I would just give it a good sharp strike like this;" and he seated himself before the "Chickering grand."

It was perfect misery to hear him. She could not endure what seemed a procession of equinoxes, storms of dominant sevenths, — universal discords to every nerve. "That's horrid!" she exclaimed at last. "Oh, do let me have some music! Such undecided nothings frighten me."

A quick glance up to her scowling face, a merry laugh, and he ceased; but that did not please her. "No," she added quickly; "don't stop there: just please resolve that last chord into the tonic. I shall wait for it."

Another laugh. "Ah! mademoiselle is *musicienne*. I hope she will not be kept waiting like the poor pianist in Prague." And then he told an amusing story of a musician, who, practising over some music, was suddenly interrupted. All day long he was busied, and could not return to the piano; and when he retired at night, tired as he was, he could not sleep. Suddenly he remembered the cause: he had been interrupted just after a note "*sensible*," and his brain was waiting for the resolution of the chord. He arose and went to the piano, struck the chord, and retired to bed to sleep soundly.

As Mr. Gottschalk spoke, he had been turning over some of his pupil's music. "Ah! here is something of Gade's, — a scherzo: come play it for me."

She drew back. "No, I am trembling all over: I can't play," she replied.

"Then watch me. Now please watch very attentively." He played the first phrases exquisitely; then he made a slight mistake (purposely, of course): but she had impulsively betrayed her surprise. She could not see his face, but felt that he was laughing at her nervousness. Then he made an absurd discord, and, springing up from the piano, said, "There, sit down, mademoiselle, and play for me. I want to look at these Passini landscapes;" and he walked to the farthest corner of the room.

She obeyed him, and never before had she played so well; for, being left entirely alone, she was relieved from nervousness.

As she ceased, Mr. Gottschalk stood beside her. "You did not finger that passage as I should have done; at least, it did not sound firm enough. Of course, I didn't see; but did not you take it thus?" and he played it, using her habit of fingering. "Now take it thus, — binding the passage in a *legato-staccato*, if I may so express it, by using the fourth and fifth fingers for the preparatory trill;" and he gave the phrase with exquisite delicacy of touch. A few more simple suggestions, and he left it for her to study, also an *étude* of Heller's; and advised her to read four or five pages from Beethoven every day, noting carefully the phrasing, but more particularly the rhythm of each measure in its beautiful completeness, yet dependent upon the following measures, "even as our Southern rhododendrons are dependent upon the unfolding of each tiny flower for the full glory of the blossom."

He looked over the music again, and, taking up the "Mendelssohn Lieder," played over the Venetian Gondola song, — that exquisite dream of a republic built amidst the murmur of the waste of waves, "set like a golden clasp on the girdle of the earth, her history written on the white scrolls of the sea-surges, worded in their thunder to gather and give forth in world-wide pulsation the glory of the West and of the East, from the burning heart of her fortitude and splendor."

The music ceased; he leaned forward, and looked at his pupil. "Tell me what you thought about while I played."

"Come to the library, and I will show you." She took up Ruskin's "Stones of Venice," and read to Mr. Gottschalk the passage quoted above; then handed him a little sketch she had once made of —

> "Only a waste of waters,
> Only a tideless sea;"

and, hovering above it in misty vision, the high altar of Torcello, and the exquisite tracery of St. Mark's glittering in the golden light of morning.

"Yes," he replied, after gazing at the sketch, "that may be the dream, but not the vision Mendelssohn saw: let me read you this passage:—

"'The greater part of the sublimity of the sea depends on its monotony. So also there is sublimity in darkness in which there is no light. Monotony, after a certain time or beyond a certain degree, becomes intolerable: the musician is obliged to break it in one or two ways; the melody harmonized, new passages introduced. Nature uses both kinds of variation perpetually. The sea-waves, resembling each other in general mass, but none like its brother in minor divisions and curves, are a monotony of the first kind; the great plain, broken by an emergent rock or clump of trees, is a monotony of the second.

"'A great man will be ready to endure much darkness of fortune, in order to reach greater eminence of power or felicity; while an inferior man will not pay the price. Exactly in like manner a great mind will accept or even delight in monotony which would be wearisome to an inferior intellect, because it has more patience and power of expectation, and is ready to pay the full price for the great future pleasure of change. But, in all cases, it is not that the noble nature loves monotony, any more than it loves darkness or pain. But it can bear with it, and receives high pleasure in the endurance of patience,— a pleasure necessary to the well-being of this world; while those who will not submit to the temporary sameness, but rush from one change to another, gradually dull the edge of change itself, and bring a shadow and weariness over the whole world, from which there is no more escape.'"

He closed the book, and hurriedly glanced at the clock. "How shall I apologize, mademoiselle? I have been so very rude as to usurp half of your morning."

"I fear mademoiselle has unintentionally detained *you*, Mr. Gottschalk," said the governess, looking up from her embroidery, and speaking for the first time. "You must punish her by not giving her another lesson this week, since she has taken the time of two in one."

"*Au contraire*, the punishment would all be mine in such case: and I don't like to suffer; my Southern n ture rebels against pain. I shall be here on Thursday, mademoiselle." With graceful reverence he left their presence; and, throwing herself at the feet of her governess, the young aristocrat exclaimed, "What a shame he is *only a music-teacher!*"

Ah! little thought that fair girl, that, eight years later, she, too, would be "*only a music-teacher*," and Moreau Gottschalk her truest, noblest friend and benefactor; and that, in her hours of despairing and discouragement, his beautiful smile would cause her to blush and laugh herself into a certain content again, as he repeated in gentlest tone, "Poor child, *what a shame she is only a music-teacher!*"

FORTE.

"Dulness and mediocrity may live unmolested and unattacked; but people never tire of finding spots on a sun whose brilliancy blinds them."

"All sound things are simple: it is the sham and rotten ones that want an intricate scaffolding to keep them from falling. The perfect arch stands without girders." — OUIDA.

VARIOUS were the comments of the Boston musical world when Gottschalk's first concert in that city was announced to take place at Music Hall, Oct. 18, 1853. Criticism must precede every thing in Boston: these shrewd people take nothing on trust; and renown, however great, won in other cities, is nothing here unless approved by those whose extremely cultured tastes and superior intellects render them capable (in their own esteem at least) of passing judgment upon *artistes* who have made a life-work of a science which those who listen have only studied to — criticise !

That Gottschalk passed triumphantly through this ordeal, the journals of that date bear ample testimony. Of course we must partially except "Dwight's;" for when is that worthy journal sufficiently unbiassed by the formalities of classical criticism to tell earnest truth from a generous heart? We would not dispute the vast musical knowledge and splendid ability of its editorial criticism: we only regret that intellectual conservatism is used in the place of the charitable, catholic spirit which should prevail among those who honestly desire musical advancement.

Gottschalk's first concert was judiciously criticised. Let the best portion of the criticism speak for itself: —

"Well, at the concert, — which, by the way, did not half fill the Boston Music Hall, owing partly, we believe, to the one-dollar price, and partly, we *hope*, to distrust of an artist who plays wholly his own compositions, — our expectation was confirmed. There was indeed most brilliant execution; we have heard none more brilliant, but are not yet prepared to say that Jaell's was less so. Gottschalk's touch is the most clear and crisp and beautiful that we have ever known. His play is free and bold and sure and graceful in the extreme; his runs pure and liquid; his figures always clean and perfectly defined; his command of rapid octave passages prodigious: and so we might go through with all the technical points of masterly execution. It *was* great execution. But what is execution, without some thought and meaning in the combinations to be executed?

"The most imposing piece of Mr. Gottschalk was called 'Jerusalem,' — a triumphal fantasia for two pianos, in the great difficulties of which he was ably seconded by Mr. J. Pychowsky, who played at disadvantage from a hastily-made manuscript copy. In portions of this there was a certain De Meyer-like pomp and breadth of harmony; but the ideas seemed commonplace, and the work as a whole left but a heavy and confused impression. There was a certain grace and individuality in the 'Savane' and 'Bananier,' which he styles 'Poetic Caprices,' though not enough to build the fame of genius on. His 'Carnival of Venice' we did not hear.

"Skilful, graceful, brilliant, wonderful, we own his playing was. But players less wonderful have given us far deeper satisfaction. We have seen a criticism upon that concert, in which it was regretted that his music was too fine for common apprehension, 'too much addressed to the *reasoning* faculties,' &c. To us the want was, that it did *not* address the reason; that it seemed empty of ideas, of inspiration; that it spake little to the mind or heart, excited neither meditation nor emotion, but simply dazzled by the display of difficult feats gracefully and easily achieved. But of what use were all these difficulties? ('Difficult! I wish it was *impossible*,' said Dr. Johnson.) Why all that rapid tossing of handfuls of chords from the middle to the highest octaves, lifting the hand with such conscious appeal to our eyes? To what end all those rapid octave passages? since, in the intervals of easy execution, in the seemingly quiet impromptu passages, the music grew so monotonous and commonplace: the same little figure repeated and repeated, after listless pauses, in a way which conveyed no meaning, no sense of musical progress, but only the appearance of fastidiously critical scale-practising."

We omit the portion where the editor doubts whether Gottschalk's forte is *composition*, and where he promises to forgive and forget all that is lacking " to place him in the rank of finely original piano-forte composers," "*if with his splendid execution he will evince the soul and fire and judgment* also " for the works of Beethoven, Onslow, &c., and turn to the criticism upon his second concert: —

"In the second concert he played some classic music, and played it well, — with clearness, delicacy, and feeling; especially the sonata for four hands by Onslow, in which he was ably seconded by Mr. Pychowsky. The surpassing beauty of his touch lent a rare beauty to these works. The 'Kreutzer Sonata,' with Mr. Suck as violinist, we enjoyed; but not more than we have done at the hands of several less remarkable pianists. There might have been more of the Beethoven fire and earnestness in opening the adagio, if they had first wrought themselves up to the true pitch of fervor by playing the first movement.

"Again: on the first night Mr. Gottschalk appeared to play with a cold nonchalance, like a merely executive virtuoso. This time his very sadness (from the news of his father's death, as well as from wounded self-esteem at missing the enthusiasm here which he had raised in Paris) seemed to re-act in the way of inspiration on his playing: there was a touch of genuine feeling, added to his grace of execution.

"Again: the few little pieces of his own which he did introduce had more charm of individuality than those he gave before; and they did not disappoint us, because they did not claim too much. They were quite unpretending, pleasing little fancies; the ballade with which he answered an *encore* was even more than that. But who could think for a moment of comparing them with such fine inspirations as any of the little mazourkas or nocturnos of Chopin; the 'Invitation' of Weber; the little tone-poems of Henselt, Stephen Heller, &c., and much more that we might name?

"His execution of Liszt's fantasia on 'Lucia,' was wonderful, and electrified his audience. But was it wise and artist-like to introduce more difficulties into the piece than Liszt had written? We *saw* the wondrous feats; but, with our eyes shut, would the music have *sounded* any better for them?"

Of this "Lucia" fantasia, "The Boston Traveller" says, —

"It was a union of all that makes music delightful, — pathos and power, sun and storm, infinite variety of expression, and almost orchestral effects.

"We sat near amateurs of acknowledged taste and wide experience in music; and we all agreed, that, as well in the Old World as the New, Gottschalk had claims to be considered at the head of his art, joint sovereign with Thalberg.

"May we not fear that the American king of music may feel no desire to occupy his throne in Boston, and that his disloyal and unsympathizing subjects may induce him to desert us for the more genial South?"

It was not these critical, cold-hearted subjects who caused him to go South. He liked Boston well enough, for he had most excellent friends and admirers there; but, for dear Music's sake, he sought a richer soil wherein to plant *his school of musical composition.*

NEW YORK, with its impulsive and generous heart, received him gladly, and enthroned him king of pianists, in reverence and love. The genial, truth-loving PHILADELPHIA welcomed him with joy; the gay, free-hearted CHICAGO hailed him rapturously. Every city throughout the Union crowned him king with homage most loyal; but *Boston* — that comically conservative, classical city, where brains appear to petrify the hearts of the people, and intellectual musical appreciation is (or rather *was*) measured on the Procustean bed of the " Journal of Music " — *dared not publicly honor him.*

To one man, indeed, do the friends of Gottschalk turn with love and reverence; for among the noblest acts in the life of Jonas Chickering, was the firm friendship and generous encouragement he ever extended to the young pianist.

During the winter of 1853–54, Gottschalk visited the Middle States and New Orleans, returning in the fall of 1855 to New York, and giving occasional concerts in Albany, Syracuse, and the larger cities in the western part of the State.

In November he went to Philadelphia. The following letter was written a short time before his departure for New Orleans and the West Indies: —

To GEORGE WILLIAM WARREN, PROFESSOR OF PIANO,
New York.

My dear, amiable, and worthy Friend, — I have had so much to do lately, that I could not answer your kind letter. The newspapers were received. I read the article, and gave it to read to all my friends, who declared that it was one of the best, if not *the best*, that had been written on me in this country. I wish I knew how to express my gratitude to you. I was in hopes that you would come to New York, and that I would have then an opportunity of entertaining you in some way or other : but I see from your last that you have changed your mind ; I am really sorry for it.

I have received a letter of invitation from a friend of mine, Zoimileny, pianist in Baltimore, who invites me to give a farewell concert in that city. He says that he has organized it, and that I cannot but do well. In Lancaster I gave one concert last week, and give my second in a few days. My intention was not to return there ; but I received yesterday an address signed by the most influential people of the place, requesting me to come and give a farewell concert.

Berlioz wrote me a long letter, which I received two days ago. He tells me confidentially some decisions of the jury (Paris World's Fair). . . .

I saw the "Prophète." It is a mere shadow of Meyerbeer's "Prophète." They have cut off two-thirds of the first act; one trio and one chorus in the second act; two choruses, two arias, and a whole scene in the third ; half a duett and the whole trio in the fourth act ; and as to the last act, it is mutilated. I do not speak of the ballets, which do not exist at all, although they are most important in this opera. The new tenor has failed completely. He has a somewhat pretty voice, but no power, and is no actor at all. He looks like a cook. Madame LaGrange is a great *artiste*. She is the one who supports alone the weight of the whole opera.

Give my respects to your mother and father, and receive for yourself, my dear friend, the assurance of my cordial and sincere friendship. Excuse my "*griffonnage.*" I was in a hurry, and wrote with a most detestable pen. My regards to our eminent, amiable, and sympathetic friend, Palmer.*   GOTTSCHALK.

PHILADELPHIA, Nov. 10, 1855.

* Palmer, the sculptor.

SENZA FORTE.

> "In the afternoon they came unto a land
> In which it seemèd always afternoon:
> All round the coast the languid air did swoon,
> Breathing like one that hath a weary dream."
> TENNYSON.

IN the spring of 1857, Mr. Gottschalk writes from Havana to a friend in New York of a brilliant entertainment given him there by the captain-general, at which banquet six hundred guests were present. His first concert was to be given the following night at the Tacon Theatre. Maretzek, who at that time occupied the house with his Italian opera troupe, resigned the use of the theatre in favor of him for one evening. To the brilliancy and success of this entertainment the journals of the day bear ample witness. A few extracts from a letter to a friend will show how earnestly he enjoyed himself.

"The sky, the air, the flowers, the fruits, are full of music to me; and, although I cannot say as much for the *ranque, unsympathetic* voices of the people, I find enough pensively-melancholy beauty in some of the faces I see to keep me in the *minore* you love so well. Especially children. How dreamily beautiful they are! Such eyes! you can look into them, and fairly lose yourself in a labyrinth more bewitching than the one owned by that cruel papa of Mademoiselle Ariadne! By the way, study the orchestration of ' Ariadne.' To me it is full of soft, seductive wiles: you can lose yourself in untying the silken braids of harmony; and when untied, and you hold them in your comprehension, it is nothing but womanly love which can weave them again. Now I recall the criticism you made on a similar harmony. Do you remember that *matinée* at the academy (the day the little lame boy brought me the tuberoses, and said he wanted to give them to me because I was *Louis Gottschalk*, and made him think of tuberoses whenever I played)? I have forgotten the theme they were giving; but I asked you how you liked the orchestration, and you said, 'It is like a

> " Swarm of fire-flies
> Tangled in a silver braid." '

Had you said '*silken*,' it would have given you my notion of ' Ariadne.'

" How I have wandered from the subject of my present surroundings, which I meant to sketch for you! I cannot say more this morning. I will write by the next steamer, unless some '*nina hermosa*' runs off with my heart before I have time to say, as ever, '*Dios te haga bueno.*' "

No " beautiful child " charmed him into forgetfulness of his correspondence with his friend; but his letters were more hurried, and filled with mere local news. In one he refers to the coming of Arthur Napoleon, speaking of him as " *un vrai musicien*," and says, —

"I wish I could be in New York to welcome him. He is a mere boy; but so bright, so full of poetic fire! He writes well, and, dearer than all to *your* heart, he plays chess well enough to checkmate your brilliant self! You could have almost as '*kaleidescopy* a conversation' as you do with me; for he speaks French, German, Spanish, and English: but whether he murders Italian as effectively as a certain friend of yours, I shall leave you to discover. Hear him, and tell me every thing you think of him *musically;* then I will write — to introduce him to you. I want you to judge him first, as you would an utter stranger. I am sorry now I've written so much about him. He is an *artiste* of the *present*."

In another letter he asks, —

"Tell me what you think of 'Chant du Soldat.' Hall will publish it soon. 'Ricordati' and 'Valse Poetique' I hope to hear criticised by your own lips; for I now expect to return before they are published."

It was six years, however, before he returned; and Arthur Napoleon did not come to this country until the following December, 1858.

In January, 1859, the musical papers published in New York, speaking of Gottschalk, tell us of his still "dallying in the fragrant islands of the West Indies." His career was one of unexampled prosperity. His presence in a town was the signal for a festival: on these occasions, from a hundred and fifty to two hundred musicians were secured to assist. It is not astonishing, therefore, that the list of his publications that year amount to the insignificant ones of " Hurrah Galop " by " *Seven Octaves*," and a few others of that sort. And here, perhaps, will be the best place to explain Mr. Gottschalk's reason for that unique *nom de plume*. He writes to a friend, —

"I think so little of these compositions" (referring to " Chant de Martyr," " Fairy-land Schottisch," " Love and Chivalry "), " that I do not care to attach my name to them. But Ditson will take them with a *nom de plume ;* so as seven octaves precede the full tone, why, I take it as the nearest approach to *my* name! Isn't that 'delicious egotism,' as you style any thing particularly absurd?"

Another cheerful letter comes from him in March, 1859 : —

" Come and breakfast with me some morning. Such chocolate, such bananas, such fried plantain! Why, you would never patronize Delmonico's again : the very memory of this tropical life would make it sacrilege 'to enter a lower sphere.' What a saving of the contents of your porte-monnaie that would be! Now, really, this life would suit you; and the *volantes* would charm you for an afternoon perhaps : but how you would scold at being prohibited your energetic morning walk! It is not *comme il faut* for ladies to walk here : but you can find exercise enough in a *volante*, and you might order your *calesero* to drive through the narrowest, roughest streets he can find (it will be an easy matter); and, if every nerve isn't braced to its utmost, ' write me down' *the animal of Dogberry's desire,* on the subject of physical exercise. Don't expect any thing about music in this letter. I am working diligently; and, next year, you shall have a musical '*Souvenir de la Havane*,' and perhaps the effect these *ojos Criollos* have upon me."

That he had worked more diligently than in former years, let the following tables of his publications witness : —

1857.
Chant de Soldat.
Ricordati.
Valse Poétique.

1858.
Grand March Solennelle.
Minuit à Séville.
Reflets du Passé.

1859.
Hurrah Galop.
Fairy Land Schottisch.
Love and Chivalry.

[These appeared under the *nom de plume* of "Seven Octaves."]

1860.
Manchega, étude de Concert.
Souvenir de la Havane.
Ardennes.
Jeunesse Mazourka.
Printemps d'Amour.
God save the Queen.
La Chute des Feuilles.
Ojos Criollos. (Duo.)

1861.
Polonia (Caprice de Concert).

FORTE PIANO.

> "Vainly for me love's signal radiance, brightening,
> Flames from her altar o'er my truant way:
> Absent from thee, the summer's harmless lightning
> Less wildly plays around the sun's last ray." — OLD SONG.

IN March of the year 1860, Arthur Napoleon joined Mr. Gottschalk in Havana, and together they gave most brilliant concerts throughout the West Indies; the principal one, at the Tacon in May, won for both *artistes* unbounded admiration.

During the summer, Gottschalk was dangerously ill, but able in August to make a professional tour throughout Central America and Venezuela. Early in October he returned to Havana, and took charge of the orchestra at the Tacon Theatre. His illness returned; and throughout the month of January he was so dangerously sick as to require the almost constant attendance of three eminent physicians. From this attack he rallied, and once more resumed his position at the Tacon, directing the orchestra with wondrous ability.

An acquaintance, writing from Cuba in November, 1860, says, —

"I heard your teacher, LOUIS MOREAU GOTTSCHALK, last night. Yes, he has all the musical ability you attribute to him; but he seems so very '*dolce far niente,*' and seems so well assured of his own powers, I do not enjoy him as much as Arthur Napoleon, or even that octave thunderbolt, Harry Sanderson. They play without *arrière pensée*, and so electrify me; but Gottschalk always sets me to thinking why he covers up his melodies with so much trimming of trill, roulade, and arpeggio. I never shall understand him, for I can't go to sleep poetically, as you and the rest of his friends do; but last night I must acknowledge he was magnificent. Of course I was head over ears in love with him, for his beautiful face and figure, as he came forward to the piano. I never saw him looking so well; and the fantasia he played was full of electric trills. I could think of nothing but our chemical lectures at school, where Prof. Hyatt touched the Leyden jar with those brass knobs, and the sparks snapped and flew about. He gave, as *encore*, the 'Valse Poétique.' You once told me he wrote it at Trenton Falls, and 'attuned it to the dash of water, and the foam-spray on the moss-banks.' I should think so: and such a dream of beauty as it is! I wish I knew him as I do Harry Sanderson. But I am terribly afraid of him, and never appear natural when he speaks to me, not even when I mention you; for he is so quiet and cool, I should think you were only acquaintances, unless I knew better."

Another letter, written about the same time, contains these words: —

"I send you a programme of Gottschalk's concert, so that you can see what I enjoyed, — that of which you have often told me. I was positively carried to the seventh heaven. Like Macbeth's witches, I vanished into thin air; and I shall never forget the *divine* impression such celestial music made upon me. Now, this is not the effervescence of boarding-school life, but the sincere milk of the truth."

What if such words were the effervescence of a fresh, girlish heart? It was to please and captivate *young* hearts everywhere that Gottschalk labored. Even if, as " the least of the disciples," he labored for dear Music's sake, it was with holiest mission of love he spoke to the outcast, and the *poor in knowledge*, of musical science. The man's mission is Christ-like, who goes into the highways and hedges of social life to gather into the Church of God the ignorant, the lame, the halt, and the blind; and, if the Bible tells us truly that music is the science of heaven, shall not the loving heart who speaks to the loiterers by the roadside, thrilling them with hope and joy, be accounted worthy higher reward than the righteous who never swerve from the beaten pathway of classic science, but preach to and teach only the rich in intellectual thought?

Be this as it may, " With my heart and life I thee worship," seemed Moreau Gottschalk's love for music. He was true to his nature, true to himself, in all these things; and the young musical world to-day is happier and wiser for his influence over sensational music, — the music which pleases the multitude.

His own words regarding his sojourn among

the West-India Islands, — the Antilles,— from the year 1857 to 1862, will give a clearer and better idea of his life-thoughts and feelings that often actuated him. They are taken from his articles published in " The Atlantic Monthly " in the spring of 1865 : —

"NOTES OF A PIANIST.

"L. M. G.

" There is a class of persons to whom art in general is but a fashionable luxury, and music in particular but an agreeable sound, an elegant superfluity, serving to relieve the tedium of conversation at a *soireé*, and fill up the space between sherbets and supper. To such, any philosophical discussion on the æsthetics of art must seem as puerile an occupation as that of the fairy who spent her time weighing grains of dust with a spider's web. Artists — to whom, through a foreign prejudice which dates back to the barbarism of the Middle Ages, they persist in refusing any high place in the social scale — are to them only petty tradesmen dealing in suspicious wares (in most instances unshrewdly, since they rarely get rich, which aggravates their position); while what they call performers are looked upon by them as mere tricksters or jugglers, who profit by the dexterity of their fingers, as dancers and acrobats by the suppleness of their limbs. The painter whose works decorate their saloons figures in the budget of their expenses on a line with the upholsterer, whose hangings they speak of in the same breath with Church's ' Heart of the Andes,' and Rosa Bonheur's ' Cattle Fair.'

" It is not for such people that I write : but there are others — and to these I address myself — who recognize in the artist the privileged instrument of a moral and civilizing influence; who appreciate art because they derive from it pure and ennobling inspirations; who respect it because it is the highest expression of human thought aiming at the absolute ideal; and who love it as we love the friend to whom we confide our joys and sorrows, and in whom we find a faithful response to every movement of the soul.

"Lamartine has said with truth, 'Music is the literature of the heart: it commences where speech ends.' In fact, music is a psycho-physical phenomenon. In its germ, it is a sensation; in its full development, an ideal. It is sufficient not to be deaf to perceive music at least, if not to appreciate it. Even idiots and maniacs are subject to its influence. Not being restricted to any precise sense, going beyond the mere letter, and expressing only states of the soul, it has this advantage over literature, — that every one can assimilate it to his own passions, and adapt it to the sentiments which rule him. Its power, limited in the intellectual order to the imitative passions, is in that of the imagination unlimited. It responds to an interior indefinable sense possessed by all, — the ideal.

"Literature is always objective: it speaks to the understanding, and determines in us impressions in keeping with the determined sense which it expresses. Music, on the contrary, may be in turn objective and subjective, according to the dispositions in which we find ourselves at the moment of hearing it. It is objective, when, affected only by the purely physical sensation of sound, we listen to it passively, and it suggests to us impressions. A march, a waltz, a flute imitating a nightingale, the chromatic scale imitating the murmuring of the wind in the 'Pastoral Symphony,' may be taken as examples.

"It is subjective, when, under the empire of a latent impression, we discover in its general character an accordance with our psychological state, and we assimilate it to ourselves: it is then like a mirror in which we see reflected the movements which agitate us, with a fidelity all the more exact from the fact, that, without being conscious of it, we ourselves are the painters of the picture which unrolls itself before our imagination.

"Let me explain. Play a melancholy air to a proscript thinking of his distant home; to a deserted lover; to a mother mourning the loss of a child; to a vanquished warrior: and be assured they will all appropriate to themselves the plaintive harmonies, and fancy they detect in them the accents of their own grief.

"The fact of music is still a mystery. We know that it is composed of three principles, — air, vibration, and rhythmic symmetry. Strike an object in an exhausted receiver, and it produces no sound, because no air is there; touch a ringing glass, and the sound stops, because there is no vibration; take away the rhythm of the simplest air by changing the duration of the notes that compose it, and you render it obscure and unrecognizable, because you have destroyed its symmetry.

"But why, then, do not several hammers striking in cadence produce music? They certainly comply with the three conditions of air, vibration, and rhythm. Why is the accord of a third so pleasing to the ear? Why is the minor mode so suggestive of sadness? There is the mystery, there the unexplained phenomenon.

"We restrict ourselves to saying that music, which, like speech, is perceived through the medium of the ear, does not, like speech, call upon the brain for an explanation of the sensation produced by the vibration on the nerves: it addresses itself to a mysterious agent within us which is superior to intelligence, since it is independent of it, and makes us feel that we can neither conceive nor explain.

"Let us examine the various attributes of the musical phenomenon : —

" 1. *Music is a physical agent.* It communicates to the body shocks which agitate the members to their base. In churches, the flame of the candles oscillates to the quake of the organ. A powerful orchestra near a sheet of water ruffles its surface. A learned traveller speaks of an iron ring which swings to and fro to the murmur of the Tivoli Falls. In Switzerland, I excited at will, in a poor child afflicted with a frightful nervous malady, hysterical and catalyptic crises, by playing in the minor key of E flat. The celebrated Dr. Bertier asserts that the sound of a drum gives him the colic. Certain medical men state that the notes of the trumpet quicken the pulse, and produce slight perspiration. The sound of the bassoon is cold; the notes of the French horn at a distance, and of the harp, are voluptuous. The flute, played softly in the middle register, calms the nerves. The low notes of the piano frighten children. I once had a dog who would generally sleep on hearing music; but, the moment I played in the minor key, he would bark piteously. The dog of a celebrated singer, whom I knew, would moan bitterly, and give signs of violent suffering, the instant his mistress chanted the chromatic gamut. A certain chord produces on my sense of hearing the same effect as the heliotrope on my sense of smell, and the pine-apple on my sense of taste. Rachel's voice delighted the ear by its ring, before one had time to seize the sense of what was said, or appreciate the purity of her diction.

" We may affirm, then, that musical sound, rhythmical or not, agitates the whole physical economy, quickens the pulse, incites perspiration, and produces a pleasant momentary irritation of the nervous system.

" 2. *Music is a moral agent.* Through the medium of the

nervous system, the direct interpreter of emotion, it calls into play the higher faculties: its language is that of sentiment. Furthermore, the motives which have presided over particular musical combinations establish links between the composer and the listener. We sigh with Bellini in the finale of 'La Sonnambula;' we shudder with Weber in the sublime phantasmagoria of 'Der Freischütz;' the mystic inspirations of Palestrina, the masses of Mozart, transport us to the celestial regions, towards which they rise like a melodious incense. Music awakens in us reminiscences, souvenirs, associations. When we have wept over a song, it ever after seems to us bathed in tears.

. . . .

"The old man, chilled by years, may be insensible to the pathetic accents of Rossini, of Mozart; but repeat to him the simple songs of his youth — the present vanishes, and the illusions of the past come back again. I once knew an old Spanish general who detested music. One day I began to play to him my 'Siege of Saragossa,' in which is introduced the 'Marcha Real' (Spanish national air); and he wept like a child. This air recalled to him the immortal defence of the heroic city, behind the falling walls of which he had fought against the French; and sounded to him, he said, like the voice of all the holy affections expressed by the word *home*. The mercenary Swiss troops, when in France and Naples, could not hear the 'Ranz des Vaches' (the shepherd-song of old and rude Helvetia) without being overcome by it. When from mountain to mountain the signal of revolt summoned to the cause the three insurgent cantons, the desertions caused by this air became so frequent that the government prohibited it.

"The reader will remember the comic effect produced upon the French troops in the Crimea by the Highlanders marching to battle to the sound of the bagpipe, whose harsh, piercing notes inspired these brave mountaineers with valor, by recalling to them their country and its heroic legends. Napoleon III. finds himself compelled to allow the Arab troops incorporated into his army, their barbarous tam-tam music, lest they revot. The measured beat of the drum sustains the soldier in long marches, which otherwise would be insupportable. The Marsellaise contributed as much towards the Republican victories in 1793, when France was invaded, as the genius of Gen. Dumouriez.

"3. *Music is a complex agent.* It acts at once on life, on the instinct, the forces, the organism. It has a psychological action. The negroes charm serpents by whistling to them. It is said that fawns are captivated by a melodious voice; the bear is aroused with the fife; canaries and sparrows enjoy the flageolet. In the Antilles, lizards are enticed from their retreats by the whistle; spiders have an affection for violinists. In Switzerland, the herdsmen attach to the necks of their handsomest cows a large bell, of which they are so proud, that, while they are allowed to wear it, they march at the head of the herd. In Andalusia, the mules lose their spirit and their power of endurance, if deprived of the numerous bells with which it is customary to deck these intelligent animals. In the mountains of Scotland and Switzerland, the herds pasture best to the sound of the bagpipe; and in the Oberland, cattle strayed from the herd are recalled by the notes of the trumpet.

"Donizetti, a year before his death, had lost all his faculties in consequence of a softening of the spinal marrow. Every means was resorted to for reviving a spark of that intellect once so vigorous; but all failed. In a single instance only, he exhibited a gleam of intelligence; and that was on hearing one of his friends play the septet of his opera of 'Lucia.' 'Poor Donizetti!' said he: 'what a pity he should have died so soon!' And this was all.

"In 1848, after the terrible insurrection which made of Paris a vast slaughter-house, to conceal my sadness and disgust I went to the house of one of my friends, who was superintendent of the immense insane asylum in Clermont-sur-Oise. He had a small organ, and was a tolerably good singer. I composed a mass, to the first performance of which we invited a few artists from Paris, and several of the most docile of the inmates of the asylum. I was struck with the bearing of the latter, and asked my friend to repeat the experiment, and extend the number of invitations. The result was so favorable, that we were soon able to form a choir from among the patients, of both sexes, who rehearsed on Saturdays the hymns and chants they were to sing on Sunday at mass. A raving lunatic — a priest — who was getting more and more intractable every day, and who often had to be put in a straight-jacket, noticed the periodical absence of some of the inmates, and exhibited curiosity to know what they were doing. The following Saturday, seeing some of his companions preparing to go to rehearsal, he expressed a desire to go with them. The doctor told him he might go, on condition that he would allow himself to be shaved and decently dressed. This was a thorny point; for he would never attend to his person, and became furious when required to dress: but, to our great astonishment, he consented at once. This day he not only listened to the music quietly, but was detected several times joining his voice with that of the choir. When I left Clermont, my poor old priest was one of the most constant attendants at the rehearsals. He still had his violent periods, but they were less frequent; and, when Saturday arrived, he always dressed himself with care, and waited impatiently for the hour to go to chapel.

"To resume: Music being a *physical agent*, that is to say, acting on the individual without the aid of his intelligence; a *moral agent,* that is to say, reviving his memory, exciting his imagination, developing his sentiment; and a *complex agent,* that is to say, having a physiological action on the instinct, the organism, the forces, of man, — I deduce from this that it is one of the most powerful means for ennobling the mind, elevating the morals, and, above all, refining the manners. This truth is now so well recognized in Europe, that we see choral societies — Orpheons and others — multiplying as by enchantment under the powerful impulse given them by the State. I speak not simply of Germany, which is a singing nation, whose laborious, peaceful, intelligent people have in all time associated choral music as well with their labors as with their pleasures; but I may cite particularly France, which counts to-day more than eight hundred Orpheon societies, composed of working-men. How many of these, who formerly dissipated their leisure time at drinking-houses, now find an ennobling recreation in these associations, where the spirit of union and fraternity is engendered and developed! And, if we could get at the statistics of crime, who can doubt that they would show it had diminished in proportion to the increase of these societies? In fact, men are better, the heart is in some sort purified, when impregnated with the noble harmonies of a fine chorus; and it is difficult not to treat as a brother one whose voice has mingled with your own, and whose heart has been united to yours, in a community of pure and joyful emotions. If Orpheon societies ever become established in America, be assured that bar-rooms, the plague of the country, will cease, with revolvers and bowie-knives, to be popular institutions.

"Music, when employed in the service of religion, has always been its most powerful auxiliary. The organ did more for Catholicism in the middle ages than all its preaching; and Palestrina and Marcello have reclaimed, and still reclaim, more infidels than all the doctors of the Church.

"We enter a house of worship. Still under the empire of the external world, we carry there our worldly thoughts and occupations: a thousand distractions deter us from religious reflection and meditation. The word of the preacher reaches the ear, indeed, but only as a vague sound. The sense of what is said is arrested at the surface, without penetrating the heart. But let the grand voice of the organ be heard, and our whole being is moved; the physical world disappears, the eyes of the soul open; we bow the head, we bend the knee, and our thoughts, disengaged from matter, soar to the eternal regions of the Good, the Beautiful, and the True."

"Written without method, dotted down carelessly, and *currente calamo*, on the leaves of my pocket-book, the notes I now publish were never intended to be read by any one but myself. A wanderer for many long years, I have contracted the habit of making daily memoranda of the fleeting, evanescent impressions of my travels, and thus giving them a more tangible form. These notes, drawn up hastily, and for myself alone, have no literary merit whatever; but they most unequivocally tell the truth. Is this an adequate compensation for the numerous negligences of style which criticism may discover in them?

"Be that as it may, these reminiscences of travel have often solaced the *ennui* and fatigue of my erratic life. In writing of the present, the bitterness of the past vanished; and again, if the present were tedious, or fraught with care, I reverted to the sunny pages of the time that is no more, and revived the sweet emotions of the long-forgotten past.

"These poor leaves have been the partners of my joys and my griefs, of my toils and my leisure, during the last three years that have whirled me relentlessly in that most monotonous yet agitated circle yclept 'a life of concerts. Should you find evidence too flagrant of the inexperience of my pen, bear in mind, I pray you, that I am but a musician, and only a pianist at that.

"*January*, 1862. — Once more in New York, after an absence of six years, — six years madly squandered, scattered to the winds, as if life were infinite, and youth — eternal; six years, in the space of which I have wandered at random beneath the blue skies of the tropics, yielding myself up indolently to the caprice of Fortune, giving a concert wherever I happened to find a piano, sleeping wherever night overtook me, — on the green grass of the savanna, or under the palm-leafed roof of a *vaguero*, who shared with me his corn-tortilla, coffee, and bananas, and thought himself amply remunerated when at dawn I took my departure with a '*Dios se lo pague à V.*" (May God reward you!); to which he responded by a '*Vaya V. con Dios!*' (God be with you!) these two formulæ constituting, in such unsophisticated countries, the entire operation, so ingeniously perfected by civilized nations, which generally is known by the name of 'settling the hotel-bill.' And when, at last, I became weary of the same horizon, I crossed an arm of the sea, and landed on some neighboring isle, or on the Spanish Main. Thus, in succession, I have visited all the Antilles, — Spanish, French, English, Dutch, Swedish, and Danish; the Guianas, and the coasts of Para. At times, having become the idol of some obscure *pueblo*, whose untutored ears I had charmed with its own simple ballads, I would pitch my tent for five, six, eight months, deferring my departure from day to day, until finally I began seriously to entertain the idea of remaining there for evermore. Abandoning myself to such influences, I lived without care, as the bird sings, as the flower expands, as the brook flows;

oblivious of the past, reckless of the future, and sowed both my heart and my purse with the ardor of a husbandman who hopes to reap a hundred ears for every grain he confides to the earth. But, alas! the fields where is garnered the harvest of expended doubloons, and where vernal loves bloom anew, are yet to be discovered; and the result of my prodigality was, that, one fine morning, I found myself a bankrupt in heart, with my purse at ebb-tide. Suddenly disgusted with the world and myself, weary, discouraged, mistrusting men (ay, and women too), I fled to a desert on the extinct volcano of M——, where, for several months, I lived the life of a cenobite, with no companion but a poor lunatic whom I had met on a small island, and who had attached himself to me. He followed me everywhere, and loved me with that absurd and touching constancy of which dogs and madmen alone are capable. My friend, whose insanity was of a mild and harmless character, fancied himself the greatest genius in the world. He was, moreover, under the impression that he suffered from a gigantic, monstrous tooth. Of the two idiosyncrasies, the latter alone made his lunacy discernable; too many individuals being affected with the other symptom to render it an anomalous feature of the human mind. My friend was in the habit of protesting that this enormous tooth increased periodically, and threatened to encroach upon his entire jaw. Tormented, at the same time, with the desire of regenerating humanity, he divided his leisure between the study of dentistry, to which he applied himself in order to impede the progress of his hypothetical tyrant, and a voluminous correspondence which he kept up with the Pope, his brother, and the Emperor of the French, his cousin. In the latter occupation he pleaded the interests of humanity, styled himself 'the prince of thought,' and exalted me to the dignity of his illustrious friend and benefactor. In the midst of the wreck of his intellect, one thing still survived, — his love of music. He played the violin; and, strange as it may appear, although insane, he could not understand the so-called *music of the future.*

"My hut, perched on the verge of the crater, at the very summit of the mountain, commanded a view of all the surrounding country. The rock upon which it was built projected over a precipice, whose abysses were concealed by creeping plants, cactus, and bamboos. The species of table-rock thus formed had been encircled with a railing, and transformed into a terrace on a level with the sleeping-room, by my predecessor in this hermitage. His last wish had been to be buried there; and from my bed I could see his white tombstone gleaming in the moonlight, a few steps from my window. Every evening I rolled my piano out upon the terrace; and there, facing the most incomparably beautiful landscape, all bathed in the soft and limpid atmosphere of the tropics, I poured forth on the instrument, and for myself alone, the thoughts with which the scene inspired me. And what a scene! Picture to yourself a gigantic amphitheatre hewn out of the mountains by an army of Titans; right and left, immense virgin forests, full of those subdued and distant harmonies which are, as it were, the voices of Silence; before me, a prospect of twenty leagues, marvellously enhanced by the extreme transparency of the air; above, the azure of the sky; beneath, the creviced sides of the mountain sweeping down to the plain; afar, the waving savannas; beyond them, a grayish speck (the distant city); and, encompassing them all, the immensity of the ocean, closing the horizon with its deep-blue line. Behind me was a rock on which a torrent of melted snow dashed its white foam, and there, diverted from its course, rushed with a mad leap, and plunged headlong into the gulf that yawned beneath my window.

"Amid such scenes I composed 'Réponds-moi la Marche des Gibaros,' 'Polonia,' 'Columbia,' 'Pastorella e Cavaliere,' 'Jeunesse,' and many other unpublished works. I allowed my fingers to run over the keys, wrapped up in the contemplation of these wonders; while my poor friend, whom I heeded but little, revealed to me, with a childish loquacity, the lofty destiny he held in reserve for humanity. Can you conceive the contrast produced by this shattered intellect, expressing at random its disjointed thoughts, as a disordered clock strikes by chance any hour, and the majestic serenity of the scene around me? I felt it instinctively. My misanthropy gave way. I became indulgent towards myself and mankind, and the wounds of my heart closed once more. My despair was soothed; and soon the sun of the tropics, which tinges all things with gold, — dreams as well as fruits, — restored me with new confidence and vigor to my wanderings.

"I relapsed into the manners and life of these primitive countries: if not strictly virtuous, they are, at all events terribly attractive. Existence in a tropical wilderness, in the midst of a voluptuous and half-civilized race, bears no resemblance to that of a London cockney, a Parisian lounger, or an American Quaker. Times there were, indeed, when a voice was heard within me, that spoke of nobler aims. It reminded me of what I once was, of what I yet might be; and commanded imperatively a return to a healthier and more active life. But I had allowed myself to be enervated by this baneful languor, this insidious *far niente;* and my moral torpor was such that the mere thought of re-appearing before a polished audience struck me as superlatively absurd. 'Where was the object?' I would ask myself. Moreover, it was too late; and I went on dreaming with open eyes, careering on horseback through the savannas, listening at break of day to the prattle of the parrots in the guava-trees, at nightfall to the chirp of the *grillos* in the cane-fields, or else smoking my cigar, taking my coffee, rocking myself in a hammock, — in short, enjoying all the delights that are the very heart-blood of a *guajiro*, and out of the sphere of which he can see but death, or, what is worse to him, the feverish agitation of our Northern society. Go and talk of the funds, of the landed interest, of stock-jobbing, to this Sybarite, lord of the wilderness, who can live all the year round on luscious bananas and delicious cocoa-nuts, which he is not even at the trouble of planting; who has the best tobacco in the world to smoke; who replaces to-day the horse he had yesterday by a better one, chosen from the first *caballada* he meets; who requires no further protection from the cold than a pair of linen trousers, in that favored clime where the seasons roll on in one perennial summer; who, more than all this, finds at eve, under the rustling palm-trees, pensive beauties eager to reward with their smiles the one who murmurs in their ears those three words, ever new, ever beautiful, ' *To te quiero.*'

"Moralists, I am aware, condemn this life of inaction and mere pleasure; and they are right. But poetry is often in antagonism with virtuous purposes; and now that I am shivering under the icy wind and dull sky of the North; that I must needs listen to discussions on Erie, Prairie du Chien, Harlem, and Cumberland; that I read in the papers the lists of the killed and wounded, that havoc and conflagration, violence and murder, are perpetrated all around me, — I find myself excusing the half-civilized inhabitant of the savanna, who prefers his poetical barbarism to our barbarous progress.

"Unexpectedly brought back to the stern realities of life by a great affliction, I wished to destroy every link that connected me with the six years I had thrown away. It was at this period that Strakosch wrote to me, offering an engagement for a tour of concerts through the United States. I hesitated an instant: one sad look was cast upon the vanished days. I breathed a regret, and — sighed. The dream was over; I was saved: but who could say, if, in the rescue, youth and poetry had not perished? Poetry and youth are of a volatile mood, — they are butterflies. Shut them up in a cage, and they will dash their delicate wings to pieces against its bars. Endeavor to direct them as they soar, and you cramp their flight, you deprive them of their audacity, — two qualities which are often to be met with in inexperience, and the loss of which — am I wrong in saying so? — is not always compensated by maturity of talent."

"*New York, February*, 1862. — One thing surprises me. It is to find New York, to say the least of it, as brilliant as when I took my departure for the Antilles in 1857. In general, the press abroad relates the events of our war with such a predetermined pessimist spirit, that at a distance it is impossible to form a correct estimate of the state of the country, For the last year I have read in the papers statements to this effect: 'The theatres are closed; the terrorism of Robespierre sinks into insignificance compared to the excesses of the Americans; the streets of New York are deluged with blood' (I very nearly had a duel in Puerto Rico, for venturing to question the authenticity of this last assertion, propounded by a Spanish officer): 'in short, the North is in a starving condition.'

"'How can you think of giving concerts to people who are in want of bread?' was the remark of my friends on being apprised of my resolution to return to the United States; and, in all humility, I must acknowledge that the same question suggested itself not unfrequently to my mind, when I discussed within me the expediency of my voyage. I have still in my possession a newspaper in which a correspondent states the depreciation of our currency to be such, that he actually saw a baker refuse to take a dollar from a famished laborer in exchange for a loaf of bread.

"The number of these trustworthy correspondents has increased in the direct ratio of our prosperity, the development of our resources, and the umbrage these blessings give to the enemies of democratic principles. There are very few governments that would not deem it a matter of duty to exult over the ruin of our Republican edifice. Fear actuates the less enlightened; jealousy is the motive of the more liberal. A celebrated statesman once said to me, 'A republic is theoretically a very fine thing, but it is a Utopia.' Like the man in antiquity, who, on hearing motion denied, refuted the assestion by simply rising and walking, we had hitherto put the 'Utopia' into practice; and the *thing did* march on and proved a reality. The argument was peremptory. A principle can be discussed: a fact is undeniable. Although refracted by the organs of the foreign press, the light of truth still flashed at times upon the people of Europe, and taught it to reflect. When our troubles broke out, I was in Martinique. In all the Antilles, — Spanish, French, Danish, English, Swedish, Dutch, — it was but one unanimous cry, 'Did not we say so?' and the truthful and independent correspondents immediately embraced this opportunity to redouble their zeal, and forthwith began to multiply like mosquitoes in a tropical swamp after a summer shower.

"But it is not my province to pronounce upon lofty political and moral questions. I would merely say that New York, for a deserted city, is singularly animated; that Broadway yesterday was thronged with pretty women, who, famished as they are, present, nevertheless, the delusive appearance of health, and brave with heroic indifference the bloody tumults of which our streets are daily the theatre; that art is not so utterly dead among us but that Maretzek gives 'Un Ballo in Maschera' to crowded houses, and Church sees his studio filled with amateurs desirous of admiring his magnificent and strange 'Icebergs,' which he has just finished.

"It is difficult to account for the extreme ignorance of many foreigners with regard to the political and intellectual standing of the United States, when one considers the extent of our commerce, which covers the entire world like a vast net, or when one views the incessant tide of immigration which thins the population of Europe to our profit. A French admiral, Viscount Duquesne, inquired of me at Havana, in 1853, if it were possible to venture in the vicinity of St. Louis without apprehending being massacred by the Indians. The father of a talented French pianist who resides in this country wrote a few years since to his son, to know if the furrier business in the city of New York was exclusively carried on by Indians. Her Imperial Highness, the Grand Duchess of Russia, on seeing Barnum's name in an American paper, requested me to tell her if he were not one of our prominent statesman. For very many individuals in Europe, the United States have remained just where they were when Châteaubriand wrote 'Les Natchez,' and saw parrots (?) on the boughs of the trees which the majestic 'Méchasébé,' rolled down the current of its mighty waters. All this may seem improbable; but I advance nothing that I am not fully prepared to prove. There is, assuredly, an intelligent class of people who read and know the truth; but, unfortuuately, it is not the most numerous, nor the most inclined to render us justice. Proudhon himself — that bold, vast mind, ever struggling for the triumph of light and progress — regards the pioneer of the West merely as an heroic outlaw, and the Americans in general as half-civilized savages. From Talleyrand, who said, "*L'Amérique est un pays de cochons sales et de sales cochons*,' down to Zimmermann, the director of the piano-classes at the Conservatory of Paris, who, without hearing me, gave as a reason for refusing to receive me in 1841, that "America was a country that could produce nothing but steam-engines," there is scarcely an eminent man abroad who has not made a thrust at the Americans. It may not be irrelevant to say here, that the little Louisianian who was refused as a pupil in 1841 was called upon in 1851 to sit as a judge on the same bench with Zimmermann, at the '*Concours*' of the Conservatory.

"Unquestionably there are many blanks in certain branches of our civilization. Our appreciation of the fine arts is not always as enlightened, as discriminating, as elevated, as it might be. We look upon them somewhat as interlopers, parasites, occupying a place to which they have no legitimate right. Our manners, like the machinery of our government, are too new to be smooth and polished: they occasionally grate. We are more prone to worship the golden calf, in bowing down before the favorites of fortune, than disposed to kill the fatted calf in honor of the elect of thought and mind. Each and every one of us thinks himself as good as, and better than, any other man,—an invaluable creed when it engenders self-respect; but, alas! when we put it in practice, it is generally with a view of putting down to our level those whose level we could never hope to reach. Fortunately, these little weaknesses are not national traits. They are inherent in all new societies, and will completely disappear when we shall attain the full development of our civilization with the maturity of age."

"My *impresarios*, Strakosch and Grau, have made the

important discovery, that my first concert in New York, on my return from Europe in 1853, took place the 11th of February, and consequently have decided to defer my reappearance for a few days in order that it may fall upon the 11th of February, 1862. The public (which takes not the remotest interest in the thing) has been duly informed of this memorable coincidence by all the papers.

"Query by some of my friends: 'Why do you say such and such things in the advertisements? Why do you not eliminate such and such epithets from the bills?'

"Answer. Alas! are you ignorant of the fact that the artist is a piece of merchandise, which the *impresario* has purchased, and which he sets off to the best advantage according to his own taste and views? You might as well upbraid certain pseudo gold-mines for declaring dividends which they will never pay, as to render the artist responsible for the puffs of his managers. A poor old negress becomes, in the hands of the Jupiter of the Museum, the nurse of Washington: after that, can you marvel at the magniloquent titles coupled with my name?

"The artist is like the stock which is to be quoted at the board, and thrown upon the market. The *impresario* and his agents, the broker and his clique, cry out that it is 'excellent, superb, unparalleled: the shares are being carried off by magic; there remain but very few reserved seats.' (The house will perhaps be full of dead-heads, and the broker may be meditating a timely failure.) Nevertheless, the public rushes in, and the money follows a similar course. If the stock be really good, the founders of the enterprise become millionnaires. If the artist has talent, the *impresario* occasionally makes his (the *impresario's*) fortune. In case both stock and artist prove bad, they fall below par and vanish, after having made (quite innocently) a certain number of victims. Now, in all sincerity, of the two humbugs, do you not prefer that of the *impresario?* At all events, it is less expensive.

"I heard Brignoli yesterday evening in 'Martha.' The favorite tenor has still his charming voice, and has retained, despite the progress of an *embonpoint* that gives him some uneasiness, the aristocratic elegance, which, added to his fine hair and 'beautiful throat,' has made him so successful with the fair sex. Brignoli, notwithstanding the defects his detractors love to heap upon him, is an artist I sincerely admire. The reverse of vocalists, who, I am sorry to say, are for the most part vulgar ignoramuses, he is a thorough musician, and perfectly qualified to judge a musical work. His enemies would be surprised to learn that he knows by heart Hummel's Concerto in A minor. He learned it as a child when he contemplated becoming a pianist, and still plays it charmingly. Brignoli knows how to sing; and, were it not for the excessive fear that paralyzes all his faculties before an audience, he would rank among the best singers of the day.

"I met Brignoli for the first time at Paris in 1849. He was then very young, and had just made his *début* at the Théâtre Italien, in 'L'Elisire d' Amore,' under the sentimental patronage of Madame R., wife of the celebrated barytone. In those days, Brignoli was very thin, very awkward; and his timidity was rendered more apparent by the proximity of his protectress. Madame R. was an Italian of commanding stature, impassioned and jealous. She sang badly, although possessed of a fine voice, which she was less skilful in showing to advantage than in displaying the luxuriant splendor of her raven hair. The public, initiated into the secret of the green-room, used to be intensely amused at the piteous attitudes of Nemorino Brignoli, contrasting, as they did, with the ardent pantomime of Adina R., who looked by his side like a wounded lioness. Poor woman! What has been your fate? The glossy tresses of which you were so proud in your scenes of insanity, those tresses that brought down the house when your talent might have failed to do so, are now frosted with the snow of years. Your husband has forsaken you. After a long career of success, he has buried his fame under the orange-groves of the Alhambra. There he directs, according to his own statement (but I can scarce credit it), the phantom of a conservatory for singing. I am convinced he has too much taste to break in upon the poetical silence of the old Moorish palace with *portamenti*, trills, and scales; and I flatter myself that the plaintive song of the nightingales of the Generalife, and the soft murmur of the Fountain of the Lions, are the only concerts that echo gives to the breeze that gently sighs at night from the mountains of the Sierra Nevada. Alas, poor woman! your locks are silvered, and Brignoli — has grown fat! '*Sic transit gloria mundi!*'"

PIANO.

> "Home again! home again!
> From a foreign shore:
> And, oh! it fills my soul with joy
> To meet my friends once more!" — M. S. PIKE.

IN February, 1862, Mr. Gottschalk returned to New York. His concert was announced for the 11th of February, the anniversary of his first concert in America. In a letter to a friend, he makes amusing comment of this: "The public have been duly informed of my arrival, and the time of my concert postponed until the 11th, as if that was any grand prestige of success; *mais que voulez-vous*, when one is in the hands of an *impressario, il faut obeir!* My friends know I am not such a dolt as to allow these things published by will of my own."

At this first concert, in Irving Hall, he was assisted by Miss Hinckley, Brignoli, Susini, Mancusi, and Mollenhauer, violoncellist. Spanish subjects seemed to possess his fancy; for his programme was filled with Souvenirs de la Havane. He played brilliantly, but some *arrière-pensée* seemed to hold his heart in check: his touch possessed wondrous *technique*, but the magnetic thrill was gone. It was but for a season: at his next appearance, before the Brooklyn Philharmonic Society, he was the same electric, dreamy, and passionate child of a tropical clime.

In March, he gave concerts in Philadelphia, and his praises were heard on every tongue. Writing to a friend, he says, —

"I'll not send you the newspapers: they will sicken you. I am glad, of course, to give pleasure; but such flattery is overdoing the matter. I go West, to Chicago, next month; but will return to New York before that, and show you some MSS. I have ready for Hall. So you don't like Polonia (*caprice de concert*)? Neither do I; but I have a poor opinion of all I do. I wish all was better. Perhaps it will be some day: until then continue to scold and criticise "Your unworthy friend,

"L. M. G."

April 14, 1862, he first appeared in Chicago, in conjunction with Carlotta Patti, George Simpson, Morine, and Carl Bergmann. The enthusiasm of his reception was characteristic of Western *whole-heartedness*. No silly hypercriticism chills true merit at the West. Fortunately for Chicago, old fogyism has been left growling at the East; and life is too short and brilliant to be wasted in picking flaws in an art which entrances them.

In May and June, Mr. Gottschalk remained in New York. One concert, however, he gave, at the solicitation of friends, in Roxbury. It was "delectable fine fun" to hear and read the criticisms his kindly consent to please his friends drew upon him. Certain critics remind us of hungry dogs, like old Mother Hubbard's who found the cupboard bare of bones; and when, from sheer sympathy, a neighbor tossed one to the starving animal, how the poor doggie growled! he didn't often get such nice rich meat to satisfy his hunger! Just so hungry, pedantic critics caught at the joyous, happy-hearted Gottschalk, and growled over him, and criticised according to classic rule and measure; thus writing themselves down the truest *Dogberrys* upon earth!

"Why will they exhaust their ten-pounders in order to kill mosquitoes?" exclaimed Moreau Gottschalk, with his merry laugh, when one of these criticisms was placed before him. "Poor Don Quixote of a critic: let us smoke a cigarette to his memory!"

The warm, sunny August days found him at Schooley's Mountains. His letters are full of beautiful thoughts, and descriptions of the scenery, the rest and refreshment he found in Nature. These letters are too personal to be of general interest; and the friend to whom they were written declines to make them public. One extract alone seems too beautiful to be lost. The letter is dated Aug. 18: —

"Your letter telling me of ——'s death saddened me all last evening; nor has the feeling passed away. I have just been thinking that the use of great sorrow and trouble may be to serve as rocks for the echo!

"Strangely enough expressed: the following is not much better: —

"Our paths lie not together!
Thine as far from mine as heaven's pure sunlight
From the cavern's gloom.
Our paths lie not together!
Mine o'er roughened rocks is traced,
My pathway smoothed by tears.
Angel-guide, with hand upon my shoulder resting,
Is it thy voice I hear?

'Tis but the breeze of heaven sighing
'Mid the am'ranth on thy brow,
Softly lingering, softly dying.
Hark! Unbroken stillness now!
Rest, rest, I give to thee.
Sister, come unto me:
Faint not, though wearily
Thou toil'st on thy way.

Clearly by thee is heard
The Mary Mother's word,
Who has for thee reserved
A heavenly home.

Weep no more; smile through thy tears;
List the music of the spheres,
Nearer rolling golden years
To still thy heart's deep pain.

Rocks retain the echo's note:
Over hill and vale will float
Clearly, though far remote,
The echo-call.

>Then if upon Life's road,
>Leading to the blest abode
>Of the Holy Triune God,
>   Rocks thee surround, —
>
>Louder still will come his voice,
>Bidding thee rejoice, rejoice
>   Sorrowing child of earth!

"It is not poetry, it is not rhyme, perhaps it is not reason: but it is the sympathy my heart holds for you; and I am not near enough to weave it into a tone-poem for your ears alone."

In October he returned to New York, and soon after went to Boston, where he gave a concert at Chickering Hall, and another at the Melodeon. Chopin and Henselt were the composers whose works he rendered; for, as Chopin had transcribed the traits of Poland to his mazourkas and Polonaise, Gottschalk had striven to reproduce the characteristic life of the West Indies in his music.

The criticism that awaited him was duly seasoned with salt-grains of justice. His playing was pronounced better than it was at his first concert, nine years before. His "Meditation Réligeuse," his "Romance d'un Martyr," were said to possess dignity of character, and impressed the critic "we" as being similar in style to the music of Ernst. Fearing, however, that this was too liberal, the just and generous critic declared that the effect of his playing was doubtless due to the superiority of the instrument!

And what said Moreau Gottschalk to this upright critique? Simply this: —

"That's a nice thing for Chickering's pianos, and I'm glad of it; for *they are grand,* and inspire me. Where's my cigar-case?"

What a comment on the pedantic, labored criticism that evidently cost time and thought to the "We" who penned it!

In November, he was once more in New York, and assisted at the Brooklyn Philharmonics. He played at one concert with Eugenie Barnetche, a young pianiste from the Paris Conservatoire; and very charmingly he kept his own wondrous power of ornamentation in check, in order to give greater scope to her power of trill and cadenza.

In December, he gave concerts in Chicago and Cincinnati. The criticism *from* this latter place seems to have been penned by a Boston "We." The daily papers were wildly enthusiastic over him; but the higher, clearer-minded correspondent of an Eastern musical journal accuses him of "descending to clap-trap" and "showy bravura." Mr. Gottschalk and his friends were as deeply affected as usual over this highly sensible effusion.

In the spring of 1863, he gave several concerts at Irving Hall, New York; but the illness of his brother, to whom he was devoted, prevented him from travelling as he had intended. He took his brother to Saratoga during the summer; but the disease, consumption, was too deeply seated to be removed by change of air and invigorating waters. In the fall they returned to New York, where, in the early part of October, Edward Gottschalk died.

During the fall and winter, Moreau remained in New York, studying music, and writing most diligently. A severe attack of fever, brought on by too constant care of his brother, prostrated him for several weeks: when he recovered, he was engaged by Strakosch for a season of concerts. Most of these were given in New York; although the finest was given in Philadelphia, where he played his arrangement from Gade's Scotch Symphony, "*Im Hochland*," with Wolfsohn. The *andante* and *scherzo* of this symphony were especial favorites of his: he compared them to "Lady of the Lake;" for the dreamful beauty of Loch Katrine was mirrored in the wave-like *tempo* of the *andante;* and the perfume of heather and gorse, the graceful swaying of the blue harebells upon the rocky slopes of mountain crags, breathed their life and beauty into the *scherzo*.

From Philadelphia, he returned to New York, where he gave a concert for the Soldiers' Relief Association. A concert in Hartford, and another in Chicago, completed his work for the year 1863. It was at this Hartford concert that another *clever* newspaper correspondent discovered in him nothing but the " Adonis of the concert-room," remarked on the manner in which he drew off his gloves, (which was very graceful indeed : this *we* is glad that that WE had an opera-glass to note things so carefully), and finally ended his *intellectual comments* by pronouncing Gottschalk " *a ninny!* "

In the spring of 1864, he left New York for a short concerting tour in Canada and a portion of the West, returning through the State of New York. It was during this tour that he refused to play " DIXIE " at a concert in Montreal. He was repeatedly encored, and a request for " *Dixie* " came from every quarter. Gottschalk went to the piano, and played " Yankee Doodle ! " To a friend to whom he related the affair, he said, " Nothing would have tempted me to play that disgraceful *secesh Dixie:* no, not if it had been to save my head ! "

In April and May, he gave concerts in Ohio and New-York State ; from Auburn he was called to New York on business that required his personal supervision. In June, he was engaged by Muzio for a concert-tour through the Middle States. They went west to Chicago, on which occasion he inaugurated Smith and Nixon's new music-hall. He was assisted by Madame Muzio (Lucy Simons), Morelli, barytone, and Doehler, the violinist.

In January, 1865, they were at Pittsburg. The following hurried note from there will show that the tour was profitable, at least: —

"You lazy fellow, did you not receive the letter I wrote you three weeks ago?

"My health is passable, though I have a bad cold. We are going down to the South-west, and will be back North in four weeks.

"Muzio is making, I reckon, from three to four thousand clear a month. Pretty good!!

"Affectionately yours in haste,
"GOTTSCHALK.
"PITTSBURG, Jan. 30, 1865."

The following list of music will show that hours of study were not neglected amid the excitement of travel: —

1862.	1863.
Pastorella e Cavalliere.	Union.
O ma Charmante (caprice).	My only Love, good-by.
Suis Moi (caprice).	Mountaineer's Song.
Murmures Eoliens.	Idol of Beauty.
Berceuse.	Slumber on, Baby dear.

1864.

Illusions Perdues.
La Colombe (Dove Polka).
Ojos Criollos (solo).
Miserere du Trovatore.
Réponds Moi (duo).
Home, sweet Home.

Overture to William Tell.
Songs.
Stay, my Charmer.
O loving Heart, trust on.

1865.

Shepherdess and Knight (song)
La Gallina (duo.)

He returned to New York in the spring, and made preparation to go to the Pacific coast with Muzio, by whom he had been re-engaged. In June, 1865, he sailed for California.

And here, in the golden summer-time, for a while we leave him sailing towards the Golden Gate, the golden Sunset Land! The sighs of parting friends cannot mingle with the *allegretto*, however *andante* the closing measures may be given. Let, therefore, the rapid movement of the *presto* come to lighten our sadness as the misty tears gather in our eyes, and we no longer note the receding vessel bearing away our dearly valued friend, LOUIS MOREAU GOTTSCHALK.

PRESTO.

" A harmony, that, finding vent,
Upward in grand ascension went,
Winged to a heavenly argument.

A harmony sublime and plain,
Which cleft . . .
            . . . those undertones
Of perplext chords, and soared at once,
And struck out from the starry thrones

Their silver octaves, as
It passed to God! The music was
Of divine stature, — strong to pass!

And those who heard it understood
Something of life in spirit and blood,
Something of Nature's fair and good."

                                MRS. BROWNING.

SENZA FORTE.

"What living man will bring a gift
 Of his own heart, and help to lift
 The tune? The race is to the swift!"

. . . . . .

"For where my worthiness is poor,
 My will stands richly at the door,
 To pay short-comings evermore.

. . . . . .

I only would have leave to loose
(In tears and blood, if so He choose)
Mine inward music out to use."

BRIGHT firelight glowed throughout the cheerful little parlor of a young music-teacher in New-York City. The gas was not lighted; but the crimson curtains and plain gilt frames of simple photographs reflected the glowing fire, giving to the room a luxuriance and beauty more subtile than any imparted by brilliant light. A bouquet of carnations and tea-roses filled a parian vase upon one side of the piano; while from a basket on the other side floated sprays of heliotrope and jasmine. A guitar lay in the crimson-velvet *fauteuil* beside the fire, and a heap of bright worsteds and canvas on an ottoman near by. At the piano sat the young teacher, weeping most bitterly. Beethoven's "Moonlight Sonate" was before her.

With head bowed in her hands, she arose and paced the room, murmuring to herself, " It is wrong, oh! very wrong, for *me* to teach: I am not worthy. It is sacrilege for a mere amateur like myself to impart the sacred mysteries of such music: it should be the work of wiser, older heads than mine, to guide the hearts of American girls into correct appreciation of the classic school." Then more bitterly she exclaimed, " How can Czerny, Heller, and Cramer *études* pave the way to purely classical music in an unappreciative mind? Chopin, too, is to them untranslatable; and most pianists are mere variationists, and have no style of their own! Oh for a *Maestro* who can sparkle out and *allure* into the glorious heaven of musical science!"

A knock at the door, followed by a low, musical voice, asking, " *Puis-je entrer?* " interrupted her. " I'm in a hurry so desperate, I can't wait but a minute."

The lady hastily wiped away her tears, and held out her hand to Moreau Gottschalk, who stood before her.

He turned her towards the firelight, and looked into her eyes. " Yes," he said slowly, " it is just as I supposed: you are in trouble!"

Without heeding her exclamations of surprise

and curiosity, he threw aside his cloak and cap, and, lifting the guitar, sat down in the chair, and quietly lighted a cigarette, saying first, "I know you do not object."

"*Mais dépéchez-vous donc, pourquoi asséyez-vous?*" the lady smilingly questioned, as she drew her little sewing-chair to the fire, and gathered up her embroidery. "I thought you were in a hurry; but, if you are going to stay, I'll light the gas!"

"I am '*going to stay,*'" he replied smiling; "because you need my society more than —— to-night." Then added gayly, "But you shall not astonish my nerves by gas-light just yet. Now confess the trouble: have your pupils persisted in playing C sharp for B flat all day?"

"No: they were all flat; no sharp to them. And yet the flattest of all has just returned from Boston, and wants *classical music*, — the 'Moonlight Sonate,' *par exemple*. But tell me: why are you here? You said, at the Philharmonic yesterday, you had an engagement every evening for a month."

"*C'est vrai, ma chere madame, mais que voulez-vous?* I stood in Hall's this afternoon as you passed; and your face was so sad, so sad, it — it spoiled my dinner: so I am here to know what is the matter."

"But you'll lose your supper-party if you stay.

I am only discouraged. I fear I am too stupid to teach. I cannot impart my enthusiasm to my pupils: they neither understand Mendelssohn nor Chopin; Listz is too hard; and if I teach *you* all the time, why, I shall be called one of your adorers, or 'Gottschalk crazy.' And I believe it is half true: I'm such a dunce, I cannot understand modern pianists as I do you. Oh, dear! why didn't I 'go on the stage,' rather than be a music-teacher?"

"Never, oh, promise me you will never think such thoughts again! *The stage!* Horrible! It would kill you. No, no. I have two more pupils for you: they shall pay you well. I know some nice music too, and will select it to-morrow."

"Indeed, you misunderstand me," exclaimed the lady hastily. "I am doing splendidly, thanks to you and ——. But I have lost confidence in myself; I've lost my interest: pupils are so stupid, or else I am. Oh!" And the hot tears streamed down her cheeks: she could not restrain them; for Gottschalk turned upon her one of those veiled, pitiful looks, so full of sympathy and childlike helplessness.

He arose and went to the piano. He played the adagio of the "Moonlight," and then modulated into soft, low strains, in which angel messengers seemed winging their way through moonlight to earth, to uphold and strengthen a fainting soul. How long he played, the sufferer never knew: she only felt the power and hopefulness of his own spirit imparted to her by magnetic sympathy; and she grew strong and radiant, upheld by his strong and happy heart.

She arose and stood beside him. "Thank you, oh, thank you, truest of friends! I am happy, self-reliant, once more. How can I ever show you all my gratitude?"

He took the hand that toyed with the heliotropes, and drew the lady nearer to him. He raised his beautiful eyes full upon her own, and replied, " I ask no thanks, but to know that you are strong and self-reliant, — to see your face no longer sorrowful, but radiant as it was before your elegant home was lost to you. Ah! you will yet find friends who will love you and appreciate you far more than those cruel, fashionable people who look down upon you because you have lost your wealth. I am honored in serving one who so nobly bears her reverses, and seeks only too conscientiously to do her duty. You know I admired you in the satins and diamonds of your wealth; but this little parlor in this unfrequented street is a thousand times more worthy my respect than the drawing-rooms of your palace home. *There* I was only your music-teacher: *here* you are my teacher. All that is good and best in my heart I bring to you; for I trust you, I believe in you."

She shook her head sadly. "Don't remind me of that wretched time when I met you as *only* my teacher. I know you now, and only regret that I dare not tell the world how grand and noble you are. Ah! will they ever find it out?"

"No," he replied decidedly: "I don't care to be known as a good or a great man. I am just simply myself,— Moreau Gottschalk; *plein d'oisiveté, la mère de tous les vices, fainéant, un peu trop amoureux des jolies demoiselles peut-être, mais* —'*ma charmante, épargnez moi.*'" He stopped abruptly; for the steadfast gaze of the womanly eyes recalled his truer self. "Well, I cannot be silly before you. I must be sensible. Let the gas be lighted, and tell me more of your trials to-day."

In a few minutes the little round table was covered with the rich materials of the lady's embroidery, and her busy needle flew back and forth, while Gottschalk leaned back in the comfortable *fauteuil*, smoking his cigarettes, and gazing into the dull red coke-glare from the grate. Suddenly he started up: "I'm going out for a few moments: I forgot something." In an instant he was gone.

"Such an erratic being! he is like an electric shock at times," exclaimed the teacher to herself as the door closed. "I wonder what he is after now? While he is gone, I'll play that 'Moonlight' as near like him as I can." She seated herself at the piano, and the *efflorescence melodique* of the adagio floated in dreamful beauty beneath her touch.

No wonder that Berlioz in his " Voyage Musicale," and De Lanz in his analysis of that sonate, has called it " one of those poetical conceptions that human language does not know how to express." In the opening of the adagio is seen " the tomb of buried hopes, the grave of love; but, as the chord of E major sounds, one hears the rustling of flowers, and feels the fragrance of their sweet breath. Though bitter tears might be shed over the tomb, though the heart might be almost crushed with the weary weight of a lonely life, the grand, solemn chords of the bass speak of courageous self-reliance, of the strength and fortitude of a truly great heart. The treble tells its passionate accents, but no human consolation can be accepted; and the deep, slow bass repeats this to the treble. Not even human sympathy: the grief must be borne in silence and alone. It is a sadness without limit, without remedy. The abyss of separation can never be bridged; a raging torrent rolls between. The soul clambers with patient firmness up the ascent without one consoling friend, and seeks the solitude of its sorrow; finding a proud content in its own self-support, in its own heroic courage."

As the final chord vibrated, a deep sigh startled the *pianiste* from her reverie. She turned: Moreau Gottschalk stood behind her. He had entered the room while she played. "Why cannot you play in that way at all times?" he asked a little severely. "You mock me. I play some things for you, which you understand as well as I do myself, perhaps better; for you know what it is to be sad, and lose every thing that makes life happy, — wealth, friends, and the one you best love of all the world; but I know nothing of all that. Come, don't play more: I don't care to be sad. I went for these: I know you love them;" and he placed before her a basket filled with white grapes and tropical fruits. "Hush! don't cry over such a simple offering: if you were in a brilliant concert-room, and had played like that, you would have been greeted with great bouquets, and I would have sent you a bunch of white camellias and violets. I would not have brought it for you all my own self, as I have this basket, for then 'the world' would have said, 'Moreau Gottschalk loves the beautiful *pianiste;*' and *les jolies demoiselles* would have been so jealous: *n'est ce pas?*" His merry laugh rang out as he lifted a bunch of grapes, and handed them to the lady. "You know I don't love anybody very long; but I love to make fun of '*les femmes savantes.*' I love cigarettes; but, more than all, I love to hear you laugh, and to see you sit down and eat grapes, and to hear you talk of *music*. Music! my only real love, the only bride I'll ever claim."

"Do not talk so, Moreau. I hope you will marry, one of these days, and give up your roving life; and may your wife be a '*femme*' sufficiently '*savante*' to appreciate you, and make every allowance for your strange, inconstant, inconsistent nature! A happy home would be a paradise for you."

He raised his eyes to her face, and replied, "Never: I shall never marry, — not by my own free will, at least; nor will any thing compel me so to do but my own conscience. Enough: let us talk of happier things." The conversation wandered to the musical news of the day, the Philharmonic rehearsals, and the concert-rooms. "Now tell me all the ugly things you've heard of me in the classical coterie at ———."

"I only tell you in order to aid you to reform. They say you are 'no artist,' only a 'musical mechanic.' You give no grand theme, only a melody overladen with ornaments of trill, arpeggio, and ' *le chant bien soutenu et lié,*' ' *canto ben sostenuto.*' Explain to me now why you are 'no artist.'"

"Because I do not follow in the track of the great schools of musical art; because I am Moreau

Gottschalk, and nobody else; because I feel joy in my soul, and let the 'tone-spirit' fly, or because I feel sad and cling to my 'tone-spirit,' striving to impart to her my heart-throbs, and calling to her from my soul in the love and despair of my passion. Music is my bride to cheer and delight me. Music is my friend to amuse and make me gay. Music — ah! it is my angel to lead me to God."

"But does it not speak in an unknown tongue to the clique at —— ?"

He smiled, and shook his head. There was sadness in the tone as he answered, "No, I think not; but it speaks of such simple things, that they understand it too well. They like those who work for the future, or those who imitate the past. They forget that I work to cheer younger musicians in their toilsome way, and, when I no longer please them, let them go higher, perhaps; but others take their place. Ah! one day I will do wonders; and you shall see me wield a baton as graceful and grand as ——: but not like him will I soothe and rest my audience. No: I'll thrill them with excitement and love; I'll inspire them with worship for my music-bride. Her *soothing* must be for me alone; and she shall *rest* me only in heaven."

As he said these words, he arose from his chair, his eyes fixed on the marble Madonna over the mantle, his hands crossed on his breast, his whole frame trembling and quivering with excitement.

"Hush, Moreau! Music in your soul can never die. For what is worthy of life in us, there can be no death."

"Go! don't speak to me now," he exclaimed, as she came near to him, and tried to lead his mind to other things. "I am tired, excited: leave me!"

"No, I will not," replied the firm, soft, womanly voice; "no, *you shall* obey me." She drew the chair back from the fire, and, taking the arm of the young artist, led him to the sofa. "Now lie down." A few gentle mesmeric touches upon his brow, and his eyes closed.

She returned to her embroidery, and worked diligently till the silver-toned clock told the hour of ten; and then she turned her head and whispered, "Moreau, Moreau, *ne dormez plus.*"

He opened his eyes, and started up. "Ah! I've been dreaming of my *fame* again. How good you are to let me rest! You must speak Italian, and say '*in sonno placido io dormiro.*' But, good-night: I know you will not let me stay longer."

He put on his overcoat, and, with the lady's permission, lit a cigar; but, before taking up his hat, he seated himself at the piano. Never did the "Miserere du Trovatore" speak in holier tones. "*Non di scorda di me,*" and "*Addio,*" rang out from a burdened, loving heart, impatiently longing, earnestly repeating, —

"Sconto col sangue mio,
L'amor che pose in te,
Non ti scorda di me, non ti scorda" —

He turned from the piano, and, bowing low, left the lady's presence without another word.

PIANO.

"Our acts our angels are." — JOHN FLETCHER.
"Large was his bounty, and his soul sincere." — GRAY.
"Good, the more
Communicated, more abundant grows." — MILTON.

IT was a lovely evening in August, and the setting sun filled the little village of Geneseo with a golden, misty haze. Young girls flitted from cottage to cottage: all seemed merry and gay, for Concert Hall was to be opened by Mr. Bassini's Normal pupils, with a private musical reception. A friend of Mr. Gottschalk, residing in the village, was one of the few who was favored with an invitation.

Three of the best piano soloists among the pupils had offered their services; and their young friends were gathering around them, urging them to play their favorite *morceaux*. "No: I will play 'Last Hope,'" replied one sweet, low voice. "If Lorette plays Thalberg, I'll follow with Gottschalk."

The passer-by shuddered, and murmured to herself, "Ah! must I hear poor Moreau murdered by school-girl attempts at music? I've half a mind not to go to-night."

Evening came, and the brilliantly-lighted hall was crowded with guests. The music was well rendered; and, when a fair girl arose from Thalberg's "Home, Sweet Home," the encore she received was fully deserved. After a charming *aria* by the sweetest and purest soprano in the class, a young girl took her place at the piano, and the opening chords of "Last Hope" filled the room with their *minore religioso*. It was marvellously well played: the girl was a fine *executante;* but there was something more than mere execution, — a soul filled with that peculiar magnetic power which Gottschalk's most earnest instruction ever imparted.

A few days after the concert, Mr. Gottschalk's friend sought an introduction to the young girl and her mother. "Is your daughter a pupil of Mr. Gottschalk?" was one of the first questions she asked. "Her rendition of the 'Last Hope' was so excellent, so like one of the composer's happiest methods of rendering it (and he had many), I felt that you must have taken it from himself."

"You are right," replied the lady; "but my daughter has never been a pupil of any one: I have been her only music-teacher. She learned the 'Last Hope' a year ago; but, after hearing Mr. Gottschalk play it at a concert last winter, she declared she never could play it again. The morning after the concert, hearing that Mr. Gottschalk was detained in town for several hours, I took my daughter to him, and begged him to give her a single lesson. He was all interest and kindness at once. I never passed a happier hour. He played it page by page, and she imitated him until she caught his idea sufficiently to carry it into her execution. He was only too generous," added the lady; "for he utterly refused any remuneration, and seemed quite shocked at the idea of my supposing he would take it. 'Are we not both teachers?' he replied, gracefully extending his hand to me: 'surely we should aid each other. Bring your daughter to New York some time, and I will aid her still more; for she has great talent, and that is something I dearly love.'"

Yes, he loved talent, but more he loved to encourage it; and there can be stories innumerable told of his generosity and self-sacrifice for the happiness of others. "Unselfish as Gottschalk" became a proverb among a certain musical coterie in New York; and to this day it is quoted when any truly great artists (too few of them, alas!) give their services as *quietly and unostentatiously* as Gottschalk ever gave his.

Where is the artist who can equal him in charities to the sick and suffering, the poor and the ignorant? In Buenos Ayres he gave concerts for the benefit of the English, French, German, and native hospitals, to the amount of twelve thousand dollars in gold. He was one of the founders of the Invalid Hospital; and all honor to the grateful hearts who presented him a golden medal for these munificent gifts! And how does he speak of it? Not in self-gratulation or glorification. In a letter to his friend, Mr. F. G. Hill of Boston, he merely says, —

"The board of public schools, common council, the directors of hospitals, and the government of Valparaiso, offered me a beautiful gilt box, enclosing a breast-pin and two dozen magnificently embroidered handkerchiefs."

They were offered, it is true, but *not accepted*. The gold medal from the Invalid's Hospital, and the beautiful set of mosaic from the ladies of Buenos Ayres, were so forced upon him by fair hands that he could not refuse their acceptance; and he ever treasured them as mementos of grateful hearts, rather than as acknowledgments of his generosity. In Montevideo he was one of the founders of the society called "Friends of the Education of the People," the object of which is the founding of public schools. Of the medals which he received, he merely remarks, —

"I have been honored with three gold medals, one of which is the gift of the ladies of the Republic of Uruguay."

But it is not so much his public charities, of which all may be assured, that we ought to speak. It is of those daily acts of kindness that distinguished and filled his life with a quiet content in the happiness of others. A single instance will show more thoroughly what such simple kindnesses were.

It was a winter afternoon of sunshine and sparkling snow-drifts; and sleigh-bells sounded their silvery tones throughout Central Park, for the roads there were splendid. Mr. Gottschalk, in the luxurious sleigh of one of New York's fairest daughters, was enjoying the drive. As the sleigh of an intimate acquaintance passed, he noticed that an invalid brother of the gentleman driving was not as usual beside him. Turning to the lady, he asked, "Where is —— to-day?"

"Much worse," she replied. "He is discouraged; fears he never will get well, and says he means to die as soon as he can. He feels he is a burden to himself and his friends."

A look of deep sadness came into Gottschalk's face: he gazed at the brilliant scene around him, and then at the hills beyond, where snow-laden cypresses pointed heavenward. After a few moments of earnest thought, he again turned to the lady, and said in a hesitating tone, as if fearing to offend, " Mademoiselle, I feel that I ought to see —— to-day. I had not heard he was worse. Will you leave me here at the corner? I will go to him at once."

It was in vain the beautiful girl offered to drive with him to his friend's house: he thanked her with the utmost gratitude, but insisted on walking. As his graceful, elegant form was seen upon the avenue, sleigh after sleigh drove up, and the fair occupants desired him to drive with them; and many were the smiles, bows, and sighs wafted to him from pretty girls and stately matrons. "This is too much: I must get out of this!" he said to a friend who had joined him. "Come, Harry, let's go into Sixth Avenue." But "Harry," who was never known to walk half a step out of his way, kept on the avenue; and it was only through some *ruse* that Gottschalk managed to leave him.

Before one of the largest confectioners on Sixth Avenue, a crowd of little ragged children stood gazing with longing eyes into the window. As Gottschalk approached them, a lady friend walking on the opposite side of the street observed him. When he reached the children, and saw the cause of their admiration, — a huge pyramid of sugar-plums rising from a foundation of cake, — and heard their envious sighs of the rich children who thronged to purchase the "*goodies*," he made his way to the shop-door, and with a pleasant smile, and "Come, you youngsters, I'll treat," he invited the crowd into the store.

The lady, who had crossed the street to meet Gottschalk, saw and heard all. She, too, entered the shop; and there, to be sure, was the young *maestro* filling the hands and pockets of the ragged crowd with sugar-plums. If he ever gave a cross look or spoke a hasty word in his life, he did on the occasion when his friend threw back her veil and exclaimed, "*Mais, Moreau, que fais-tu parmi les bonbons?*"

"*You* here! ah, you *spy!*" and he actually blushed as if caught in an ungentlemanly act; but continued, " I am only on a little *folâtrerie*, — a harmless *petit soupé, à la Maison Dorée, pour les enfants*. But, come: these poor children are too full to speak. Let us go."

Full or not, the ragged crowd gave a parting cheer that was more grateful to his kind heart than the *bravos* of the concert-room.

"You are real good, Moreau. But how comes it you are in this part of the world alone?"

In a few words he explained the cause, and added, " I was going to stop at your rooms and get a book to read to ———. What shall I take?"

" Adelaide Procter, or Tennyson, if you like."

" Yes, I'll take Adelaide Procter: I like that best. And I'll read ' Give me thy Heart.' There is a breath of music all through that poem: you hear the organ-notes die away, and the voices of spirits speaking in the shadowy gloom of evening." They walked on in silence for a while; and then he exclaimed suddenly, "Ah, well! why isn't it just as well to be a heap of sugar-plums as an applauded musician?"

"What *are* you thinking about?" questioned the lady in an amused tone.

"Only this: if I were sugar-plums, the little children would like me and admire me, and I could make them happy."

"But you make older ones happy now."

"Do I really? or is it only that they make themselves happy in thinking I serve them?"

"You mean they arrogate to themselves your power of pleasing. For instance: a beautiful woman favors you, honors you with delicately scented *billets-doux*, pets you ' *en faisant les beaux yeux:*' you feel she only admires you because you have striven to please her; not because she knows your inner nature, and apprehends you *yourself*."

"Exactly. You know I don't belong to myself before the world: I am in the employ of the manager who engages me, and I must do all I can to attract fine audiences: therefore I must ' *faire les beaux yeux*' in return, and allow myself to be petted, flattered, and caressed."

"Oh, you absurdly arrogant creature! How you must suffer! how you must dislike to resort to such deception!"

"Please do not pretend to misunderstand me," he said, as he looked down into her upraised eyes with his sad but radiant smile. "It is all very nice indeed: I'm a man, and I like it immensely. But you know what I mean: it does not satisfy me; it is not the pure, childlike love which my soul craves; it is a *made-up sentiment,* with which sympathy and kindred tastes have nothing to do. What do you suppose I care for the sentimental trash of these women, any woman indeed?"

"But, Moreau, you couldn't live without their caresses!"

He turned upon her a glance of anger like a lightning flash. "What do you suppose *life* is to me, if you really think that true? Life for *me* must be *love;* but not the sort of love a woman who flirts with me can give. Life must be gay and bright, but bright with my own deeds of helpfulness to others. Life must be for some *end and aim;* and you know what *my* aim is, — to aid and cheer those who listen to my music, to interpret the good I feel in my own heart to those striving as I have striven. I may fail; but I shall do my best to be true to myself and to the science for which I live."

"Moreau, are you true to yourself when you hide your real nature from the world? So few *really* know you."

"But *my friends* do," he replied quickly,

"and that is all I ask: and I hope, if I am generous and charitable, my example will be followed by others; and if they, in their turn, do all the good they can, why, I think the world will be none the worse for the indolent, *dolce far niente* life of Louis Moreau Gottschalk."

Noble, generous child of those glorious tropical climes where no cold "calculating costs" comes to check the generous impulses of the heart! In that day when the crown-jewels of a Saviour are made up, when the recording angel reads from the golden record the names of those who have "loved their fellow-men," ah! methinks the name of **Louis Moreau Gottschalk** will be foremost in the van of that glorious company; and the music of heaven will be stilled while the words, which, eighteen hundred years ago, were spoken in Judæa, will re-echo throughout the golden summer-land, —

"Inasmuch as ye have done it to one of the least of these my brethren, ye have done it unto **Me**."

FORTISSIMO.

> "On dit que dans ses amours
> Il fut caressé des belles.
> Qui le suivirent toujours,
> Tant qu'il marcha devant elles."
> BERNARD DE LA MONNOYE.

"Man delights not me; no, nor woman neither." — SHAKSPEARE.

A DARK November day had hung over New York; and the city was damp, chilly, and mournful. The crowd of carriages, with their elegantly-dressed occupants, were rapidly driving home from Central Park; and every face looked blue and cold in the fast-gathering light of evening. On the steps of one of the most elegant mansions in Fifth Avenue stood Moreau Gottschalk.

He had lighted his cigar, and was wrapping his graceful Spanish cloak more closely about him, when he caught sight of a lady who passed the house and turned into Twenty-third Street. In an instant he was beside her. Throwing away his cigar, and taking the music-roll she carried, he offered her his arm, saying, "It is too dark for you to be walking alone. Come, I will go home with you."

"No: it is your dinner-hour, and I can take the cars in Sixth Avenue."

"Now be quiet, and don't talk any more. I was coming to see you, even if I had not met you; for I have much to ask you."

There was such hesitancy and doubt in his tone, that the lady looked up to his sad face, and asked quickly, "Are you ill, Moreau?"

"No: only tired, '*discouraged*' as you say. I know," he continued, not heeding her expression of surprise, "it is not from over-exertion in teaching, for that is not required of me by the pupils I've had to-day; but it is so hard to talk sentimental musical nonsense to amateurs who are not even appreciative, save from rote, — some musical, nonsensical criticism they've learned."

"Why do you talk to them, then?"

"How can I help it? When a sweet, pretty woman looks at me, and asks a sensible question about music, I answer her from mere impulse; and so am often drawn into a half-and-half flirtation; for, of course, that is all I attempt."

The lady laughed. "Ah, Moreau! when do you attempt whole flirtations with your sincere friends, — myself, for instance?"

"No," he said very quietly. "I never attempt to storm a battery so much stronger than myself. I should have my own guns turned against me in the first onset!"

"*Trève de compliments*, Moreau," and the lady laughed aloud. "Your answer is characteristic, and I'm ashamed of myself for suggesting such a strain of talk."

His merry smile re-assured her, and he said, "It isn't in human nature to talk sense all the time; and I know I should consider you rather *inhuman*, ' *strong-minded* ' perhaps, if you did. *Mais voilà, nous sommes chez vous*: no, I'm not coming in just yet," he said, as he handed her her music-roll. "I will be here at eight o'clock. And don't make any other engagement for the evening: I am going to take you somewhere with me. Eat your dinner in peace, and don't be curious." He lit another cigar, and turned towards Broadway.

The nine-o'clock bell at City Hall had sounded, and still Moreau Gottschalk sat in the velvet *fauteuil* in his friend's parlor. On the ottoman beside him, her arm resting on his chair, sat the lady, pleading as only a woman can plead with a wayward, obstinate child. "Moreau, what earthly pleasure can it give you to go to those '*petits soupers*'? It is not the kind of excitement that you ought to indulge in. There are plenty of sweet, good women in the world."

"*O mon Dieu! yes*," he exclaimed: "*un peu trop!*"

"Now, hush! I mean there are plenty of quiet

home-bodies, who never appear in public; and surely they could make an evening pass pleasantly to you" —

She paused: his amused laugh silenced her; and he answered, "My dear young woman, who knows best what is good for me? — you who never went to an *artiste* supper at Maison-Dorée in all your life, or myself? True, I can pass my evenings pleasantly enough all alone; my music and my reveries are more entertaining than any thing I can find away from my own room: but I need the *laisser-aller* of the companions I meet tonight; and — yes, I may as well tell the truth — the badinage and repartee of those you call *actresses* and *artistes* are so far superior to any thing I hear in *la haute société*, that it wakes me up, and amuses me when weary."

"I am sorry you know so little, then, of *la bonne société*," she said in rather a hesitating tone. "Perhaps it is wicked to say it: but somehow these *soupers d'artiste* remind me of *demi-monde;* and that frightens me. I know there is a brilliancy and sparkle that can only come from gentle birth and intellectual culture, — exceptions innumerable, I grant you: but, after all, *la bonne société* is like the river fed with pure mountain springs, although those springs may have risen from the black earth, and trickled through moss-banks; while *demi-monde* is the *aqua fontana* of chemists, brought through pipes, pumps."

"*Do* please say *filters*," he exclaimed with his merriest laugh. "I only want your absurd sentiment to get you into a trap; for you know filtered water is the purest. But never mind: I know what you mean better than you do yourself; and I'll not turn your own word-weapons against you. To me, *demi-monde* implies artificial society, worldly women, intriguantes, adventuresses, and those whom common sense cannot approve: but, after all, they are *women;* and you know what Burns says, —

'What's done we partly may compute,
But know not what's resisted.

I shall shock you, I suppose, if I tell you, that, in Europe, I've met queens of *demi-monde* who were intellectually superior to the women who honor me with concert-room or philharmonic rehearsal flirtations; and you know some of these belong to *la bonne société* in New York!"

The lady was silent, and rose to look over the evening papers on the table; but Mr. Gottschalk motioned to her to sit down again. "I know you are getting angry, and I rather like it; for it isn't often you do a silly thing. Now, you know I intend to go to Madam ———'s supper at la Maison-Dorée to-night, and intend to take you with me."

Like a flash of lightning the lady sprang from

her chair and stood before him. "How *dare* you, Moreau?" But tears checked her utterance: with a cry of pain she sank on the floor, and buried her face in her hands.

He too had risen, the dreamy look gone from his eyes, a proud, indignant expression rendering them far more beautiful. He raised the half-kneeling woman, whispering softly but sternly, "Hush, Octavie: do *you* dare to doubt me, — *you* whom I love as my sister, *you* whose child I have held to my heart as a little brother? By the memory of that angel-boy, listen to me."

With face suffused with tears and blushes, she faltered, "Forgive me, Moreau: I never doubted you; only I forgot that I am now only a music-teacher in our *bonne société*, and must mingle more with the *artistes* of my profession. I know" — she paused again, tears came so fast; "I know Madam —— does not belong to *demi-monde;* but she used to sing at my *soirées* professionally. She was not an invited guest."

"And why not?" he asked coolly, as he drew a *fauteuil* towards the lady, and leaned against the mantle with folded arms. "Was she not equal to you in good sense, superior to you in beauty, if not in grace? was she not ladylike? Ah! this boasted equality in republican America — what a myth it is! But come; I'll not discuss the question: you don't know how to argue. 'We'll agree to disagree.' One thing I'm certain of: you're a born aristocrat."

" Yes, thank God! " flashed out the lady.

" Don't become heroic: you'll eclipse Ristori," he said with cool sarcasm. " Every true woman is an aristocrat: self-respect and truth make the gentlewoman, not clothes nor culture. If your ancestors did hold rank in the Court of Lady Washington, are you any more ' *sang pur* ' than the good little maid who sweeps this room ? "

" No; but more *sang froid*, and capable of reminding Moreau Gottschalk that even my regard for him will not allow me to listen to what I deem his impudence."

" *Cela m'est égal*," he replied with perfect indifference, and walked to the piano. A few strangely wild arpeggios rippled from the keys; abrupt modulations rushed into a demoniac polka; a tornado of anger swept through the wild measures: but still the small voice of conscience occasionally trilled far up in the treble, and in doubting, hesitating chromatics, came down at last into the passion and anger of the surging bass, stilling its wild rage. Suddenly he started up, and the next moment was kneeling beside the lady's chair; like a tired child he came with tearful eyes, and whispered, " Madre, forgive me: I did wrong to anger you. I know I am right on my side the picture, and I am sure you are right on yours. One of these days you'll come over on my side, and see that I am right: till then I can only wait in patience."

"Moreau," and the lady laid her hand on his beautiful brow, "I, too, was angry and rude: I need your forgiveness. I know I have self-respect and truth, but cannot yet

'Smile at the claims of long descent.'

You who know the world so well, and know just what women are, help me to be a true, noble woman, whether aristocrat or plebeian."

"There spoke my brave, splendid Octavie again!" he said, springing to his feet, and taking her hand. "Come, let us play '*Réponds-moi!*'"

And they went to the piano. Such a merry, laughing *duo* as it was! Those delicate, beautiful hands of the *artiste* flew here and there, in and out, improvising trills and roulades of exquisite melody. It was a *danse cubaine* to the trilling of birds, amid plant-orchestration of tropical hue, and perfume of the forgetful Egyptian lotus sweeping over the souls so lately filled with anger and strife. At its close he turned to his friend, and with soft, low tones full of persuasion, said, "You will go to Maison-Dorée with me to-night? *Réponds-moi.*"

"Yes, I will," she answered.

"That is right. Now you have half an hour to appear *en grande toilette*. You are too *distinguée* in that plain black; you look like an empress in disguise: but in colors you look like other women. Now go and dress, please, and come down closely veiled. The carriage will be here at eleven o'clock. But wait: before you go, I want to tell you that I do not *smile*

'At the claims of long descent;'

although I hold to the belief that

'Kind hearts are more than coronets,
And simple faith than Norman blood.'

I do like those born of a long line of patrician ancestry: they are more refined, more quickly susceptible to the sympathetic spiritual needs of their friends, than those new to culture and social rank."

"Ah, Moreau! I forgive you entirely."

The blue-room at la Maison-Dorée was never lighted for a merrier party of artists and pianists than that given by Madam —— in honor of a splendid concert success lately achieved by a fair *débutante*. Three of the most brilliant journalists were present; and although their wives and daughters were quietly at home, doubtless pitying the business that detained the "father of the family" in the editorial chair, these poor business-men were full of amusing witticisms, and provoked most brilliant repartee from the fair *artiste* by whom they were entertained. It must be confessed, there was a moment's hesitation and awkwardness when the door opened to admit Gottschalk and his friend; for she was an utter stranger to Madam ——, who had invited her at Gottschalk's request. The embarrassment was but momentary; for Gottschalk, in mirth-provoking manner, caught up a liquor-glass, and, filling it with champagne, poured a few drops on her head, saying, "*Soyez le bienvenue, Octavie, reine des chromatiques.*"

It was impossible not to laugh, and the laugh silenced questioning; and she was never known to any except as "Octavie, une Française, l'amie de Gottschalk."

What a gay, merry night it was! Most delicious viands covered the table, and choice wines sparkled in delicate glasses. Art and music were the topics of conversation; and many a brilliant criticism flashed out under the exhilarating influences of Cliquot, and "Sunshine" equal to that of Monte Béne. Gottschalk, although at the head of the table, was not the leader in these wild but merry tales: he listened, and smoked his cigarettes, or toyed with the fruits before him, his eyes fixed on his friend, who sat at his right, also quiet, but amused, and enjoying the new social sphere into which she had entered.

"'*Reine des chromatiques*,'—what does that mean, Monsieur Gottschalk?" asked one of the ladies on the other side of the table. "Is mademoiselle *vocaliste*, or *pianiste?*"

"Both," he replied smiling. "So, of course, she is all tones combined, rests nowhere; but flashes and sparkles like 'La Source,' which, by the way, —— played so finely at your concert;" and so he turned the conversation from his friend. But it was of no avail: in a few moments the lady returned to the charge.

"She sings, I am sure: such a rippling laugh as that designates a soprano."

"Ah! what a faultless art critique you are!" retorted Gottschalk, laughing. "Just listen, and say no more." He led "Octavie" to the piano. "You must sing, to quiet and satisfy them," he whispered. "They are mystified enough. Come, what shall it be? I want your grandest contralto tones: then you shall go home; for I know you must be tired." All this was said as he improvised an exquisite minore prelude to Bassini's "Soledad," arranged for contralto.

It was impossible to hesitate or falter, upheld by such accompaniment: the applause her execution received was due more to the *pianiste* than to her own merit.

"Well, am I foolish, or not, to waste my time among such associates?" he asked, when they were seated in the carriage again.

"No: if every supper-party is like this, I think it is recreation for you."

"But for yourself, how do you like it?"

"Oh, not at all!" she exclaimed, shuddering. "I prefer my own little room, my books and my piano, to all the men and women in the world. For myself, such evenings would be silly waste of time. I would rather read that bad Grenville de Vigne, or listen to your absurd flirtation stories *de Paris*, than participate in any such scene. But with you it is different: I think it wakes you out of your dream-life. You may go whenever you please. And now, good-night; for here we are at my home."

As he handed her from the carriage, and accompanied her up to the door, he said, "Thanks for your permission. But I don't care for suppers: I had much rather go to bed and have a good night's rest; my health demands it. But I was determined you should attend a supper, and so know how to criticise the actions of your gentlemen friends when you hear of 'midnight orgies' at 'Maison-Dorée,' or any other 'Maison.' To-night was a fair sample of *my 'orgies bachchanale'!*"

"In the presence of women you mean?" questioned the lady.

"Ask my gentlemen friends how much worse I am with them. I know I am happier with them; and, knowing that, you should remember '*La charité se réjouit du bonheur d'autrui.*'"

"I had better remember that '*Les plus sage ne le sont pas toujours.*'"

AGITATO.

"None knew thee but to love thee,
Nor named thee but to praise!"

"When hearts whose truth was proven,
 Like thine, are laid in earth,
There should a wreath be woven
 To tell the world their worth.

. . . .

It should be mine to braid it
 Around thy faded brow;
But I've in vain essayed it,
 And I feel I cannot now.
While memory bids me weep thee,
 Nor thoughts nor words are free,
The grief is fixed too deeply
 That mourns a man like thee."

OCT. 25, 1863. I have just copied the above verses. Moreau Gottschalk gave them to me last week. His sad face to-day, as he passed me on the avenue, recalled them. I fear his poor brother Edward is worse."

The foregoing paragraph, taken from an old journal, seems aptly fitted to introduce the following sketches gathered from conversations with friends who were frequently with Mr. Gottschalk during the spring, summer, and fall of 1863.

"I remember the day Gottschalk expected his

brother. It was in the early spring of 1863, — a damp, raw afternoon. He asked me to go with him to the steamer, somewhere down by the Battery, I believe. As a Bostonian, I do not know enough of New York to be sure of the direction we took: I only know, that, when we reached there, we were told that the vessel was detained at quarantine, and it was not known when it would arrive.

"The next morning, however, while Gottschalk was receiving some friends at his boarding-place, his brother came. 'Take Edward up to my room, please,' he said to me: 'I will follow immediately.'

"I ran up stairs, quite forgetting how weak and ill poor Edward was. When we reached his brother's room, he could hardly speak: his breath was gone. I led him to the sofa, and he lay down. Gottschalk, entering soon after, went to him, and, putting his arm around him, sought to amuse him by conversation. He was too weary to speak, and only said, 'Play for me.'

"'Yes; play "Berceuse,"' I suggested: 'Edward has never heard it.'

"Gottschalk went to the piano, and, with all the pathos and soul-power of which he was master, he gave that exquisite cradle-song, almost the lullaby of death into life eternal; only holding the loved one to earth by the lingering love-kiss of the closing measures, — those pure, sweet measures, freighted with the passion of a mother's kiss upon the eyelids of her sleeping darling!

"How it called up the mother-love in the hearts of those long-parted brothers! Clasped in each other's arms, Moreau and Edward Gottschalk wept such tears as only pure-hearted, earnest men weep, — tears that assoil the soul of sin, tears that 'drop like amber' while the heart cries out for that

> 'Divinest voice complete
> In humanest affection;'

even God's blessing, that they might

> 'Lose the sense of losing.'"

The summer days came on; and the brothers went to Saratoga, hoping that the medicinal waters and the dry inland air would benefit the declining strength of the young invalid. Moreau Gottschalk was untiring in his devotion to his brother. He drove out with him when able to ride; but most of his time was passed in his brother's room, reading to him, and amusing him by every means in his power. It is true he was often seen in the parlor, playing for the guests: it was the only way he could return the many kindnesses shown him and his brother by the fair inmates of the hotel. What if these beautiful women thronged about him? was it a mark of unmanliness to receive their sweet adulation? However much they may have wearied him, — for weary him they did, — he rarely manifested his weariness: he was at all times a perfect gentleman.

One evening, however, when flattery and praise had fairly sickened him, he whispered to a friend with whom he was playing a *duo*, "I can't endure this any longer. I must go: Edward needs me;" and so he left the thoughtless crowd, and shut himself in his brother's room, utterly refusing to go to the parlor again.

But he did not deny his friends the delight of hearing his wonderful improvisations. At night, after the dancing was over, and the guests had gone to their rooms, Gottschalk and a few friends would come down to the parlor of Union Hall, and there he would play for them. Delicious moments, never to be forgotten! When hours flew by, and the moonlight faded from the long corridors, and the stillness of midnight reigned over all, out on the calm night-wind floated strains of melody, freighted with the red wine of love poured out in the golden silence of the soul's sympathy. Again and again the rich purple hue of suffering swept athwart the heart, and the *minore* deepened into harmonies of amethystine splendor; but the day-star of hope rose silvery clear in the Orient of the poet's soul, and flung its luxuriant radiance over the passion of the contrite, purple sadness.

> A seraph, bending from his sphere,
> Marvelled such tones should linger here:
> He stilled his harp, then caught the strain,
> And bore it home to heaven again.
> Thus memory echoeth the tone
> That love once breathed for love alone!

All too quickly flew by those summer hours, and the September days found the brothers once more in New York. The coveted strength had not been granted the invalid; and very soon Moreau Gottschalk knew that his brother must die. What pen can paint the anguish of that loving heart! His own words but dimly shadow forth his grief. The following hurried note to a friend,* written during a season of great suffering, must tell its own story: —

DEAR ——, — I have not written to you this long while, on account of poor Edward's illness. He is fading away gradually, and, alas! will leave this world for another — better, I hope — ere the week is over. The doctor tells me to-night that he may perhaps not last so long; that at any moment he may — I cannot write the dreadful word!

You can imagine my feelings better than my pen could ever describe them. Adieu, dear F——.

Yours truly and sadly,
GOTTSCHALK.

WEDNESDAY, 10, P.M.

* To Mr. F. G. Hill of Boston.

Edward Gottschalk died, and Moreau was left alone. The winter came on, and quietly and sadly Gottschalk devoted his time to the study and practice of his art; his chief recreation being the companionship of his musical friends. He rarely appeared in public. Occasionally he looked in at the Philharmonic rehearsals, when Beethoven's music was given. One afternoon, the "Eroica" was played. Gottschalk was sitting beside a friend, in an obscure part of the house. As the magnificent orchestration of the "Marche Funèbre" resounded throughout the academy, he leaned his head on one hand, every nerve in his body quivering and trembling as with pain. All through that glorious apotheosis to a heroic soul his breast heaved with convulsive sobs, only suppressed by strongest self-control. His friend slipped her hand into his, whispering, "*Ayez pitie de moi, Moreau : vous savez bien que je souffre.*"

It was her only hope of arousing him, — appealing to his generous nature. His hand closed on hers with an iron clasp; and in a voice choked with tears he replied, "Oh, help me to bear it! I am very weak. This music is agony. No hope! no hope! O Edward, my brother!"

But the music —

> "A strain more noble than the first
> Mused . . . and outburst.

> With giant march, from floor to roof
> Rose the full notes; now parted off
> In pauses massively aloof,
>
> Like measured thunders; now rejoined
> In concords of mysterious kind,
> Which won together sense and mind!"

As the closing measures, throbbing with the noble despair of proud hearts, sank into silence, he raised his head, his pale face glowing with a look almost unearthly in its expression of peace, and said, "Forgive this selfish sorrow. Ah, Beethoven! again thy voice is leading me. I will conquer." Then, for the first time becoming conscious of the poor little hand he had bruised in his strong clasp, he looked into the face of his silent companion with an expression of bewilderment, as sad as amusing. "Let us go," was all he said. "I have been a brute to make you suffer so."

"I have not felt the pain before this moment, Moreau. Like you, I suffered mentally; but, unlike you, I have not heard Beethoven's voice guiding me into nobler, more generous life-duties."

"You have no need of Beethoven: you are beyond his comfort; you hear a voice that I do not always hear, — the voice that Mrs. Browning asks in the lines, —

> 'Speak low to me, my Saviour, low and sweet;
> From out the hallelujahs sweet and low.'"

"Go on: recall the next lines, and you, too, will hear that voice, —

'Not missed by any that entreat.'

Ah, you have heard it: but it came to your *artiste* soul in the pulsing of the music; and —

> 'As a child,
> Whose song-bird seeks the wood for evermore,
> Is sung to in its stead by mother's mouth,
> Till, sinking on her breast, love-reconciled,
> He sleeps the faster that he wept before.'"

"Sleep is very sweet, then, if this comfort I now feel be sleep. I only hope it will last me till I awake in the better land."

"Sleep? Ah, no, Moreau! it is the awakening to a life of nobler endeavor; and you must work, —

> 'Make clear the forest-tangles
> Of the wildest stranger-land.'"

"Hush! I must be more practical; I must 'make clear' a pathway for piano-music. I have begun by publishing such descriptive pieces as 'The Banjo,' much to the disgust of those who think I can't do better, and condemn me for debasing my genius. But what care I? I know the method by which I intend to develop a love for piano-music. It is an ungenerous nature who cannot 'stoop to conquer.' If I condescend to be attractive to the less intellectually appreciative, I will make them love me, and so follow me while I lead them step by step higher. I am willing to bear criticism; for, before I die, I am convinced my music will be appreciated, whether my motives are or not."

"You shall be rightly known one of these days, Moreau; for the few who know you now will never suffer you to be misunderstood. But so live, my dear friend, that

>'When the summons comes,'

you will be

>'Sustained and soothed
>By an unfaltering trust.'"

"I will. How could I be unfaithful to those who know and love me? I shall die at work; I feel sure of that. Oh! I hope now it is not far off: I am so weary of life!" And his beautiful eyes filled with tears; he pressed his lips firmly together, and, after a few moments' silence, continued: "No, that is wrong: I have work to do yet, and *I will conquer.*"

FINALE.

The finale is like the teeming waves of lava flowing from Vesuvius. The flame darts up from the summit of this glorious mountain-sonata; the thunderous explosion sounds; then there is a halt; and then pours from the volcanic breast of the poet all the solitary moan over the bitter absinthe-draught contained in his dark goblet of life. — DE LANZ: *Analysis of The Moonlight-Sonata.*

"Now thou art blessed in some celestial air
  Whose calm effulgence floods the jasper sea.

. . . . .

I know 'tis surely so: heaven's splendors rise
From thy dissolving tabernacle's wreck.
Oh might they flash in vision on these eyes!

. . . . .

When shall it be? . . .
  How many trailing seasons shall it be
Before I tread with thee the sphery way,
  And the deep things we talked of scan with thee,
  Drinking the morning stars' triumphal symphony?"

CON SORDINO.

"They are never alone that are accompanied with noble thoughts."
                                                    SIR PHILIP SIDNEY.

"Love thyself last; cherish those hearts that hate thee:
Corruption wins not more than honesty.
Still in thy right hand carry gentle peace,
To silence envious tongues; be just, and fear not.
Let all the ends thou aim'st at be thy country's,
Thy God's, and truth's." — SHAKSPEARE.

"L' injure se grave en métal,
Et le bienfait s' écrit en l' onde."
                                        JEAN BERTRANT.

FROM the Golden Gate of San Francisco, a vessel sailed southward to the Chilian coast, bearing to the heart of the tropics one whose genius glowed with the fervor and brilliancy of that southern clime.

Away from an envious and jealous throng sailed the ship; from those who sought by shameful slander to shadow the fair name of a noble, generous man: and Moreau Gottschalk, unconscious of the lying reports creeping towards the North, went southward to gladden music-loving souls of a sunnier land. Ah! could he have known the cruel stories which wounded and angered the true-hearted friends he had left in the United States, he would have returned at once and faced his calumniators: but before letters from friends, urging his presence in New York, reached him, it was too late to return; his engagements forced him to remain. It made little difference: what cared he for the rude rabble whose own evil hearts led them to believe a lie? His friends knew him and trusted him, and soon traced out the slanderers. And what reply made Gottschalk when he heard it?

In a private letter to a friend are these words: —

"It is beneath my dignity as a man of honor to notice such slanders. Surely my friends can never credit them; and, if believed by those who are not my friends, I only pray kind Heaven give them better minds. A man whose nature allowed him to commit so dishonorable an act could also lie, and disown it! Let the story of my whole life be told, every act scrutinized; and, if you can find in it any thing to prove me capable of such unmanly conduct, cast me from your regard, blot my name forever from your memory."

Let these manly words silence forever the dastardly attempt to injure a noble soul.

When the thunderous applause of crowded concert-rooms is for a moment hushed, again Moreau Gottschalk turns his loving regards to his Northern friends; and the following simple notes will show how little his trustful heart doubted their friendship: —

To Mr. F. G. Hill of Boston.

Dear H., — This may interest you: I am in good health, concerts successful, longing to go back to the States, often thinking of dear old friend Hill.

Have composed lots of pieces for piano, violin, voice, &c., besides two symphonies for orchestra, two cantatas and choruses, one grand march dedicated to the Sultan, a triumphal hymn to the Emperor of Brazil, a tarantella for piano and orchestra, dedicated to the King of Italy.

In Peru I gave about sixty concerts; was presented with a gold, diamond, and pearl decoration. In Chili the government voted me a grand gold medal. The board of public schools, the common council, the board of visitors of hospitals, and the government of Valparaiso, each presented me with a gold medal.

. . . .

Please let me know how you are. I feel always the same towards you. Time and absence never change my sentiments towards those I once have loved; consequently I am *always* your friend.

If you ever write, direct

"L. M. Gottschalk, al cuidado del
   Senor Agustin de Castro,
    Montevideo Republica del Uruguay."

A hearty shake-hands.
    Yours as ever,   L. M. G.

Montevideo, April 14, 1869.

To Francis G. Hill, Professor of Piano, Boston.

Dear Old Hill, — Last night, at ten, I got your kind letter dated Feb. 5. Need I say how pleased I was to hear from you?

Thanks for the notices in papers. I hope you will occasionally keep the friendly portion of our public posted up about poor old Gottschalk, who is and has been ill used very often, and is certainly not half as bad as some would make him to be.

Chickering writes me that Strakosch is anxious to have me go back to the United States, and offers me an engagement, which, so far, I have not accepted.

. . . .

My latest compositions, written within the last three months, are three Études de Concert, one Impromptu, one Scherzo, a Septuor, a Capriccio, and several Lieder.

Write to me soon; letters from the North are such a happiness to me.

Ever faithfully your friend,
GOTTSCHALK.

This is all he tells of the laurel wreaths crowning his brow; but from "The Montevideo Standard" (El Siglo), Oct. 9, 1868, the following is taken: —

"MR. GOTTSCHALK IN MONTEVIDEO, — D. José P. Varela has had the kindness to communicate to us the following charming letter from the celebrated Gottschalk, in which he offers to give a concert in favor of the 'Society of the Friends of Education.'

"We know not whether we please or displease Mr. Gottschalk by saying, with our habitual frankness, that his letter, be it considered as a literary production, or in reference to the doctrines which it advocates, rivals the best compositions which he ever conceived for his magic instrument.

"To the thoughtful, there is as much pure harmony in these sincere and enthusiastic lines, inspired perchance by the remembrance of his country, which we endeavor to ennoble and take as a model among us, as may be found by the *dilletanti* in his select compositions, 'La Muerta,' or the 'Murmullos Eolicos.'

"And for us poor hunters of an ideal which continually escapes us, Gottschalk gains more prestige by thus revealing himself in this new character, than on the scene of his triumphs; entrancing all hearts by the combination and force, united to the sweetness of the torrent of harmonies which spring from his hands in obedience to the inspiration and genius of the artist.

"The offer of Mr. Gottschalk, for the rest, is most important; and it is proper to warmly thank this noble American citizen for the material aid which the society is about to receive."

The following is the letter of Mr. Gottschalk : —

MY DEAR SIR AND FRIEND, — The kind invitation you sent me has afforded me the pleasure of hearing the eloquent speeches which you and Dr. Carlos Maria Ramirez delivered upon "Popular Education," — a subject so important, and of such vital interest to the progress of the new American nations.

It befitted you, who studied and understood the institutions of my great and beloved country, to imitate this noble undertaking, and to transmit to the Oriental youth, of whom you are one of the most distinguished representatives, with the enthusiasm of your generous convictions, the result of your observations in the United States.

"Let us enlighten the masses," you rightly said, "and we will purify them."

And, certainly, of all the forms of government, the republic is that which exacts from the people the greatest degree of enlightenment: under it each citizen ought to actively participate in its destinies; as he constitutes, so to speak, a fraction of the government itself.

Those favored by fortune can educate themselves in all countries: and it is for that reason that the American thinkers did not dedicate their cares to the aristocratic element of society, but rather to the lowest ranks of the great mass of the people, whom they have struggled to enlighten; comprehending that education ought not to be a privilege, but something which belongs to all, as much as the air we breathe; and that every citizen has as imprescriptible a right to the light of the Spirit as he has to the light of the sun which illuminates him.

The popular system of education in the United States, in that austere elaboration, which, of a child, makes successively a man, and later a citizen, has, for its principal object, to prepare him for the use of liberty, — that cuirass of the strong, but which frequently, for the weak, is transformed into the shirt of Nessus.

In my country, it is not its eminent individuals, but the superiority of the intellectual level of the people, which attracts the attention of the observer; for, however great Prescott, Longfellow, Everett, Bancroft, and many others, may be, these noble characters are lost to view in presence of the enlightenment of the collective entity, — the "people." It is of great interest indeed to our political existence and to our prosperity, that the most obscure of the farmers of the "Far West" can lay aside the plough to ascend the tribune, and spread abroad from thence the most patriotic and progressive ideas.

But I perceive, sir, that I am repeating badly what you have already said with so much talent.

I was among the first to sign my name on the list of the "Friends of Popular Education;" but a sterile adhesion is not enough for a work which demands material efforts to overcome the obstacles which prevent its realization.

I therefore offer you a concert, in benefit of the association of the " Friends of Popular Education."

Later, others will come, who, perhaps, stimulated by my example, may offer you a more efficacious assistance; but I can assure you that none will be animated by wishes and sentiments more sincere than those of your friend,

Louis M. Gottschalk.

However severely the ignorant may assail Moreau Gottschalk's character at the North, there were those in South America who knew his worth and noble deeds.

The following is the reply to his letter from a Directory who knew how to appreciate and reward noble acts and great artists: —

Montevideo, Oct. 14, 1868.

Sir, — The Directory, through the means of one of its members, Mr. José Pedro Varela, has been advised of the noble and generous offer with which you kindly favor the society of the " Friends of Popular Education."

The name of Gottschalk, inscribed on the first record of the society, filled with satisfaction the original commission; and now the Directory, composed in great part of the same persons, sees with pride the same name of Gottschalk associated with the first manifestation of public aid that the society receives after its installation. The great idea of the education of the people, the beautiful ideal of self-government, which counts you among its sons, inspires our humanitarian association. In view of your disinterested and spontaneous offer, the society could imagine, that, in some measure, the great Republic sends it her approval and her aid, through the organ of her glorious and enlightened artist.

The Directory accepts with pleasure and enthusiasm your generous offer; and its secretaries are charged to arrange with you the method of carrying it out.

In the name of the society of the "Education of the People," the Directory fulfils its duty by expressing to you the profound thankfulness with which your noble conduct inspires it, and takes this opportunity to salute you with the expression of its highest consideration.

ELBIO FERNANDEZ, *President.*
CARLOS M. RAMIREZ, *Secretary.*
PEDRO JOSÉ VARELA, *Secretary.*

TO MR. LOUIS M. GOTTSCHALK.

Not only in Montevideo, but in Buenos Ayres, were his noble charities most freely given. Then it was that he determined upon his festival of three hundred and fifty musicians. "The Montevideo Standard" gives the following extracts: —

[*Tuesday, Nov.* 10.]

"For the whole of the last fortnight, the only topic of conversation was Gottschalk's great festival, in which over three hundred persons would take part. Everybody was looking out for seats; and such was the demand, that, yesterday morning, all the localities in the spacious Solis Theatre were already sold.

"Reports of persons who had assisted at the rehearsal gave to understand that the concert would prove a very great success; but, raised to an extraordinary degree though the expectations were, the reality yet surpassed them by far.

"The theatre was filled with a select and elegant audience; nearly all notabilities, both native and foreign, being represented.

"The festival commenced with Verdi's 'Traviata,' sung by the Italian Opera Company; and, after a short pause, the curtain rose again, and Gottschalk appeared, greeted by the warmest applause.

"It cannot be our intention to speak again of Gottschalk's eminent qualities as a pianist. Everybody who has heard him, and who has not had this good fortune, knows that he has few rivals throughout the whole world. Of the three pieces which he played on Chickering's piano, we have to point out his 'Faust Fantasie,' — one of the richest gems of his composition, full of the most melodious notes and the most wonderful harmonious combinations.

"At last the third part of the concert commenced, — the real festival! Over three hundred persons filled the stage. Nearest to the audience were the pianos, stringed instruments, flutes, clarionets, oboes, &c., leaving in their midst an elevated platform for Gottschalk. At the back of the stage, on an amphitheatre, were the drums and brass instruments.

"When the opening chords of the march from 'Le Prophète' began, the audience seemed electrified. Such sonorous music was never heard before; and how admirably was the enormous orchestra conducted by Gottschalk! That he did it without having before him any *partitura*, is scarcely to be wondered at, in a talent like his; but still, what a memory must he have! Not once during the whole concert had he any music lying before him.

"In the 'Prière from Moïse,' the chorus of ninety persons was admirably effective; and this masterpiece of Rossini's found general applause. The two last numbers on the programme were Gottschalk's own compositions, — 'Marche Solennelle,' and 'Montevideo.'

"Gottschalk may well be proud of the triumph which he obtained last night. What immense difficulties of all kinds he has had to overcome, what incessant work he had to do for the last two weeks, nobody can imagine; and well does he deserve the praise of being the man who has given the greatest and most successful concert ever heard in this part of South America. May he, in his brilliant career, remember now and then his grateful and sincere admirers in Montevideo! When shall we hear again an artist like him?

"His work may better be imagined than described, when it is known, that, although Chili is the country of music-makers, from the highest to the lowest orders, not an eighth part of the musicians he engaged could either read or write; and not a fourth part of them knew a note or character of music, and yet 'Tannhauser,' 'Le Prophéte,' and 'Fidelio,' were perfectly familiar to them."

In the spring of 1869, about May 10, he went to Rio de Janeiro.

Echoes of the thunderous applause his genius won in the concert-rooms of Rio soon reached his friends at the North. His own letters give so simple and pleasing an account of these triumphs, it will not be wrong to quote from them: —

To Mr. F. G. Hill, Boston.

My Dear Old Friend, — My concerts nere are a perfect *furore.* All my houses are sold eight days in advance.

Boxes in the hands of speculators (you may judge if they are alive) bring seventy-five dollars premium, and single seats twenty-five dollars.

The emperor, imperial family, and court never missed yet one of my entertainments.

His Majesty received me frequently at palace. He is very kind to me, made me sit near him. We chatted last time over an hour and a half. The *Grand Orient* of the masonry of Brazil gave me a solemn reception. A deputation was appointed to wait on me.

The enthusiasm with which I have been received here is indescribable. At the last concert, I was crowned on the stage by the artists of Rio, headed by my dear and much-talented friend, the great Portuguese pianist, Arthur Napoleon, whom you, no doubt, remember as one of the most successful artists who visited the United States.

The emperor is very fond of my compositions, especially "Printemps D'Amour," and "Ossian."

My "Morte" (she is dead!) has had here, the same as in the Rio and La Plata, *un success de larmes*, as several of my fair listeners wept at listening to that rather sad and disconsolate of my last effusions, which is my favorite now, and which I consider as being neither better nor worse than old "Last Hope."

My fantaisie on the national hymn of Brazil, of course, pleased the emperor, and tickled the national pride of my public. Every time I appear I must play it.

In great haste, yours as ever,

GOTTSCHALK.

Rio, June 22, 1869.

To Mr. F. G. HILL, BOSTON.

My dear H., — Although you did not reply by this packet to my last letters, I suppose you have them, since I received a letter from ——. Thanks. My concerts are just now over, on account of Ristori having the monopoly of the theatre in which I was giving them; but as soon as she leaves, which will be soon, I will resume my entertainments.

The San Pedro College tendered me a reception, which was *quite an affair.* The young men (six hundred), with bands, flags, professors, priests, ladies, &c., drawn up in a line, welcomed me in a most enthusiastic manner. I was marched into the HALL processionally, played for them, was cheered, &c.

There was afterwards a banquet (about three hundred guests at the table). A beautiful speech was made by one of the *Honors* of the University, to which I responded amidst hurrahs and cheers.

"*The Prosperity of the Great Republic of the United States*" was proposed by the president of the college; to which I, of course, was bound to answer. My speech was, I suppose, less bad than those I am called upon to make so often; for it was published in the papers, and praised by some writers, political and literary. It was about education, free schools, the duties and rights of citizens, &c.

On the 30th, the emperor gives a grand fête at the palace, at which I am to play. I see his Majesty very often. He is a very kind and liberal-minded man. He is fond of inquiring about the States; and we have long talks together, alone in his private apartments.

As ever,   L. M. G.

RIO, July 24, 1869.

To MR. F. G. HILL, BOSTON.

Dear H., — I am recovering slowly. Of course I do not yet feel strong; but, thank God! I am in good health. I receive occasionally the papers you are kind enough to send me.

The papers in the Rio Plata have had me dead lately. The fact is, that, on the 5th of August, I was so low (yellow fever) that my physicians gave me up. The emperor, who had constantly shown me the greatest kindness since my arrival, as soon as he knew of my sickness, sent every day *officiously* (? !) one of his chamberlains to inquire after my health; but, on the 5th of August, he ordered his first gentleman in waiting to call on me officially. At half past eight in the evening, a court carriage stopped at my door; and, a few minutes afterwards, the chamberlain in full court uniform stood at my bedside. Of course I could not speak, and hardly understood what was going on; the fever being so intense that I had been delirious, singing, and making political speeches, during four consecutive nights and days.

Notwithstanding my being unconscious, the courtly gentleman, in his glittering tail coat, delivered solemnly the imperial message, and, after remaining half an hour in my room, returned to the palace. All this I heard of when the fever subsided. As soon as I could stand on my feet again, my first visit was for the emperor to thank him for the kind interest he and the empress had shown me.

I gave a concert night before last, crowded: it is my seventh in Rio. The next one takes place day after tomorrow. After that, I give a new series, with orchestra and thirty pianists; and at last, for the *bonne bouche*, three grand festivals, with eight hundred performers, at which I will produce my symphonies, and the grand "Marche Triumphale" I dedicated to the emperor. He is very anxious to have those festivals organized, and has offered me the means to muster in Rio all the musicians that can be had within the province.

If you can speak of all this in the papers, you will please me much, as I would like our people to know that there is *one* emperor who is not a tyrant, and who likes the Americans.

In great haste, but yours as ever,
GOTTSCHALK.

Rio, Sept. 24, 1869.

To Mr. F. G. HILL, Boston.

Dear H., — No time to write. Received musical papers, in which I read some notices of my doings, no doubt emanating from the gifted pen of F. G. H.

Am preparing grand festival, eight hundred musicians; new symphony to be performed under my baton.

The emperor has issued an order to secretaries of war, navy, and justice, by which I am appointed, *pro tempore*, director-general of all the bands of national guards, army and marine. I have already three hundred and seventy-four men working. Five hundred more await my orders. Just think of eight hundred performers and eighty drums to lead.

Yours as ever, in great haste,
L. M. G.

Rio, Oct. 24, 1869.

VALMCA, 22d Aug., 1869.

To OLIVER DITSON, Boston.

My Dear Sir, — I have been very ill, and feel very weak yet. My physicians say I have had the yellow fever: all I know is, that I suffered much, and was very near emigrating *from* this planet to parts unknown. Thank God, it is all over now; and I give — although still in a very dilapidated condition — a concert to-morrow night.

I had heard of Gilmore's great undertaking. I am glad he succeeded. I accept your offer, &c.

. . . .

My sister, Clara Gottschalk, has sent me lately the manuscripts of some of her piano compositions, which are remarkably pretty and taking. I have no doubt they will become popular, because they are not difficult, and their style is peculiarly elegant, with a touch of feminine sensibility and poetry which cannot fail to please the masses.

I have not heard for three months from friend F. G. Hill. I hope he is not sick. As ever,

Yours truly,
GOTTSCHALK.

To Messrs Hall & Son of New York, he writes, —

RIO, Oct. 24, 1869.

Herewith I send you a new piece ("Morte," — "She is Dead"), — a lamentation. I do not know whether it will be successful or not, but I believe it to be my best effort for years. Ever since I have played it, it has been encored; and a great many women have hysterics and weep over it — maybe owing to the romantic title. However, here it is. Please beg your engraver, for common-sense' sake, to pay some attention to the orthography of the French indication and to the title. He has given me so often proofs of his complete unconcern, interpolating all sorts of nonsensical words of his own invention, that my request ought to be taken into consideration.

I am preparing a festival for eight hundred performers; will lead myself, and have performed several new works of my own composition. I have been appointed by his Majesty director-general (temporarily) of all the bands of the army, navy, and national guards. An order from the emperor, issued to the secretaries of the navy, justice, and war, has been issued, communicating his intention that I am to be obeyed. In great haste, yours always,

GOTTSCHALK.

SAN ISIDRO, OCT. 24, 1869.

To GEORGE WILLIAM WARREN, Professor of Piano, New York.

My dear George, — Ashforth leaves to-morrow for the United States; and I avail myself of the opportunity to remind you of your old friend G., who, although silent, never forgot you, and is just as sincerely your friend now as he has ever been for the last fifteen years.

One of the first names which came to my memory when I saw Ashforth was your own name; and glad I was to hear that you were doing splendidly, and were always as great a favorite amongst the profession and with the upper-tendom.

As for myself, you know pretty much all I have done since I left the United States. I went to Peru whilst civil war was raging; was at the battle of Lima when the city was stormed by that black-hearted, half-breed, ignorant, savage dictator Prado. In Chili I organized, after having given sixteen concerts in the capitol (Santiago), several festivals of four hundred and fifty musicians, which I led, and had several of my symphonies performed. The Government decorated me with a gold medal. I then gave several concerts for the hospitals, and afterwards a series of performances for the benefit of the public schools. The Board of Instruction of Santiago presented me with another gold medal, as did also the "National Society of Lima:" this last medal is ornamented with pearls and diamonds.

In Buenos Ayres, Valparaiso, Montevideo, &c., &c., I was also decorated with gold medals, diplomas of membership of academies, institutes, &c., &c. Having given for the building of the German hospital one concert in Buenos Ayres, which netted over sixteen thousand dollars, the Board of Directors agreed that my name should be inscribed on a marble tablet in the lobby of the establishment.

My new compositions are very numerous. They are as follows: two books of Études de Concert: two symphonies for orchestra; one "Marche Héroïque," dedicated to the emperor of Brazil; also, for orchestra, six mazurkas de concert, six waltzes de concert, about a dozen of bravura pieces, a score of melodies, nocturnes, romances, and a grand Tarantella for pianos and orchestra, which is my "cheval de battaille," as it is called for at all my concerts, and always encored. This last piece I have dedicated to H. R. H., the princess of Savoy; and I received lately a letter from Count ―― (I forget his name), minister of the king of Italy, in which he assures me that I am to be made very soon a companion of the new order of Italy, " La Stella d' Italia," and that the cross of knighthood will be sent me.

I am ashamed of myself, after looking over these badly-written four or five pages, and discovering that I have done nothing but speak of myself. Well, my dear George, you must excuse me, and see in that *Ego*-tism a proof of my faith in your friendship.

How many children have you now? Please write me soon and lengthily, as nothing can give me more pleasure than hearing from my United-States friends, and especially from you.

Within four weeks I expect to be in Rio, where papers say that I am to be well received.

I was delighted, and so were you, I am sure, to hear of our friend Chickering's triumph in Paris. His pianos deserve, undoubtedly, all their fame; and here they are becoming the rage since I have made them known. Is Albert Wood still at Steinway's?

If you see our excellent and most respected friends, Mr. and Mrs. Sidney Mason, please give them my best and kindest regards. Tell Mrs. Mason I intend sending her my photograph very soon (also to you).

Adieu, my dear old fellow: I send you mentally a hearty shake-hand. My respects to your wife.

GOTTSCHALK.

How full of enthusiasm and honest pride are these lines, — the last, alas, he ever penned to his friends at the North!

Faithfully and earnestly he worked to make this festival the grandest ever known in Rio. Faithfully and earnestly, giving out his magnetic strength to inspire with his own genius those who were lacking, or slow to win perfection in performance. Weakened by long illness, during the burning summer, his nervous system excited and wrought to highest tension, he worked on. We know not what divine strength may have been vouchsafed him; but God, in his mercy, granted him his heart's desire, and the vision he had seen in the little parlor of his friend "Octavie," in New York, was realized.

On the evening of the 26th of November, the long-expected festival was given. The Opera House was crowded, and the entire imperial family was in attendance.

"The music was superb. The 'Marche Solemné,' which he had composed and arranged for the entire orchestra, and dedicated to the emperor, was the last and crowning piece of the evening. It was received with such manifestations of approval as one rarely witnesses in a life-time. When, towards the close of it, was heard the well-known strains of the national hymn, which were so beautifully interwoven with the original theme of the composition, the effect upon the audience was electrical. All sprang to their feet, and the wildest enthusiasm prevailed. This was one of the proudest moments of Gottschalk's life. Again and again was he called to the front of the scene, and it was long before the audience finally dispersed. This proved to be the last concert that he was destined to give, — the fitting completion of a great career."

The following day he was too ill to rise from his bed; but when evening came, rather than disappoint his audience, although suffering intense pain, he exerted his iron will, ordered his carriage, and went to the Opera House.

The thronged house greeted him with shouts of joyous welcome; but alas! the beautiful brow was flushed with pain, and the white lips could only murmur regrets and excuses for inability to lead his orchestra that night. He returned to his hotel; and Dr. Severiano, one of the best physicians in Rio, took charge of him.

About the 8th of December, he was removed to Tijuca, a *plateau* about two or three miles from Rio, where change of air promised to restore his strength. At first, there seemed reason to hope that recovery was possible: the violent internal pains decreased; but his weakness was so great, that after an operation, which caused some relief, he gradually sank, and, at four o'clock on the morning of the 18th of December, breathed his last. On the afternoon of the same day, his remains were removed to the hall of the Philharmonic Society, where he had touched the piano for the last time; and there, under the direction of his physicians, Dr. Severiano, Rodriguez Martins, and Dr. Costa Ferrar, his body was embalmed.

The love and almost reverence in which Gottschalk was held is fully shown by extracts from the journals of the capital. The following is from the " Journal da Tande " of the 18th instant: —

"The great artist is dead. At four o'clock this morning, after prolonged sufferings, Gottschalk breathed his last, victim of that art to which he had consecrated the choicest years of his life. One more Levite for the temple of immortality, one more star to shine in the firmament of the elect of God. The sepulchre may conceal his body; but it cannot hide his name, which not even coming ages shall have the power to destroy.

"Still are sounding in our ears the echoing harmonies of that final concert, last song of the dying swan, solemn and majestic as the sound of his own fame. Son of that giant country which will yet dictate laws to the world, Gottschalk was a universal celebrity.

"Geniuses have no fatherland. In speaking of great poets, the world is their country and all ages claim them. He was born in America; and, though he had visited many lands, fate still destined that on American soil he should find his last resting-place. Gifted with rare endowments of intellect, not less conspicuous were the qualities of his heart.

"The muse of Gottschalk was ever employed in the noblest of objects. To alleviate suffering was with him a constant practice, as it was also his delight. How many times has it dried the tears of orphans? How often has it tempered the grief of the widow? Many concerts were given by him in aid of different benevolent societies, and the numerous medals which he had received were the most convincing proofs of his charity and intelligence. The public, then, of this capital should go to-morrow to pay the debt of gratitude they owe to Gottschalk, shedding unfeigned tears upon the tomb that is to enclose the remains of a great man."

In the early dawn of morning, news reached the city that Moreau Gottschalk had passed away from earth! Everywhere upon the Rua Ovador, the *Palais Royale* of Rio, groups gathered to mourn over the death of one whom all loved. Behind the shaded lattice of many a house, gentle hearts beat sorrowfully, and beautiful eyes were weeping; for he whose glorious music had thrilled them with joy and hope had gone forever from their sight!

With earnest respect and loving admiration for his genius, the Philharmonic Society, the oldest and most important musical association in the city, claimed the privilege of arranging his funeral. We are told that, —

"One of their number, a distinguished surgeon, with several assistants, promptly and successfully performed the operation of embalming; and, on the 19th, the body was exposed in state in the front hall of the society until the time of commencing the funeral ceremonies, when it was removed to the interior and larger hall, where were assembled the principal mourners. Before removing the body to the cemetery, the orchestra of the society played one of the great artist's favorite compositions, entitled 'Morte.' At this moment, the scene was most solemn and impressive.

"As the deceased was a Roman Catholic, the ceremony was conducted with the usual rites of that church. After some brief service read over the body at the doors of the society, the cortège moved on. The coffin was preceded by a band of music, which at intervals played the solemn strains of a dirge. The funeral car was not brought into requisition at first; but the artist-friends of the dead, among whom were seen Arnaud, Ellena, Lambert, Wagner, Cavallo, and Arthur Napoleon, competed with each other for the sad privilege of bearing with their own hands his precious remains. Immediately after, in two long lines, came the mourners and friends, uncovered, and carrying in their hands lighted torches. The route of the procession, which passed in this manner as far as Largo da Lapa — the distance of perhaps a mile — was crowded on both sides by the populace, who paid the greatest respect to the cortège as it passed. The coffin having been placed in the funeral car upon its arrival at the Lapa, it was borne directly to the cemetery of San Juan Baptista, in Bota Fogo, distant some five or six miles, followed by hundreds of the mourners in carriages. All along the road the highest marks of respect were being constantly shown. The cemetery itself was found thronged with people, anxious to have one last look at the face of the deceased. But only a few enjoyed this privilege. When the coffin had been placed within the little chapel, and opened to remove the medals and decorations, — now worn for the last time, — it was permitted to gaze once more upon the well-known features of the dead. Two brief and fervid orations, in accordance with the custom of the country, were then pronounced by the side of the open coffin, amid the profoundest emotion. The scene was most impressive. The sombre aspect of the place, lighted only by flickering torches; the ghastly features of the dead; the trembling voices of the speakers, and the unfeigned grief of all, — combined to make it a scene never to be forgotten."

The following appeared in the " Reforma " of the 21st instant : —

" The funeral of Gottschalk was a splendid public manifestation. The Philharmonic Society had claimed the honor of guarding the precious remains of the great artist until the time of burial. It was an act of consideration and artistic fraternity, which honored alike the society and the country. The body was embalmed at the expense of the same society, by Dr. Costa Ferrar, who gratuitously offered his services.

" Day before yesterday, up to the hour of the ceremony, the body lay in state in one of the principal halls of the society, appropriately decorated. Near by was seen, covered with crape, the piano upon which Gottschalk had played for the last time, on the night of the 25th ult. Previous to removing the body, the orchestra of the society performed the 'Morte,' one of the most beautiful and touching compositions of the great artist. The coffin was carried by hand as far as Largo da Lapa, preceded and followed by hundreds of persons of all classes bearing torches. A band of music led the way. The street and squares were crowded. Sadness marked the faces of all, and many eyes were bathed in tears.

" In the Cemetery of San Juan Baptista, the press of people was even still greater. Here, in the midst of profound emotion, was spoken the last sad farewell to the remains of one of the greatest artists of our time. Dr. Achilles Varejao and the distinguished academician of La Paulo, Señor Antonio Cardoso de Manezes, made themselves the interpreters of the general grief. They spoke with trembling voices, and were heard amid tears.

"The following facts regarding the last moments of the great artist have been communicated to us: At midnight he predicted that within four hours he would be dead; and he died at ten minutes to four the following morning. He wished to make some testamentary dispositions; but he had not the strength to sign what he had ordered his secretary to write. Two unmarried sisters, who reside in London, are the heirs of his fortune, which consists of property in the United States, and certain funds left in the hands of persons in his confidence.

"He leaves many unpublished works, including three operas, one of which — *Isaura de Salerno* — was his favorite composition, and upon which he constantly worked to perfect it. His intentions were, upon leaving Brazil, to give a series of concerts in the United States, and afterwards to go to Europe and bring out his unpublished compositions, and then make a journey to Palestine to visit the holy places, as he had promised his mother to do when she died."

And the promise would have been kept: for through the long summer evenings when watching at his brother's bedside in Saratoga, again and again he referred to that promise, and cheered his brother with thoughts that together they might wander among the hills of Palestine; and at such times the exquisite imagery of his imagination would picture the scenes he so longed to view. The oleanders on the banks of Jordan, the wild luxuriance of the hills about Jerusalem, were vividly pictured to his young brother, and such dreams of beauty as his words inspired soothed and calmed the fainting heart of the dying one.

But we sorrow not as those without hope, over the wealth of heart and mind God has taken from this cruel world. Music is the science of heaven; and Louis Moreau Gottschalk, in that he has done what he could upon earth, shall find a nobler sphere of action in the presence of the angels of God.

TEMPO PRIMO.

"They tell me I am shrewd with other men.
  With thee I'm slow and difficult of speech:
With others, I may guide the car of talk;
  Thou wing'st it oft to realms beyond my reach.

. . . . . .

For them I wile the hours with tale or song,
  Or web of fancy, fringed with careless rhyme;
But how to find a fitting lay for thee,
  Who hast the harmonies of every time?"

. . . . . .
JULIA WARD HOWE.

MANY beautiful tributes to Gottschalk's memory are lying before me: it would not be kind to close these memoirs without notice of them. First among them I find the following pages from Madame Clara M. Brinkerhoff.

She prefaces her "Sketches" by a note to Madame Hensel, in which she says, —

"I enclose some recollections of my dear friend, that may differ somewhat from those you have on hand. Our acquaintance was one that drew out the highest and best of a man's nature, the recognition of soul to soul. No length of time or space could blot out one iota of a friendship formed, as ours was, on mutual respect and esteem.

"My acquaintance with Mr. L. M. Gottschalk dated from about the year 1854.

"At our first meeting, our conversation, instead of finishing in a few moments, as would have been natural under the circumstances (a piano-room introduction), lasted for more than an hour and a half. I knew that I had met a man of genius and high culture.

"He recognized in me one who could read his better nature, which he so often chose to hide under the semblance of a man of gallantry, whose highest aim was to please, and gain woman's bright smiles for himself, — or a certain sort of patient demeanor, which said, 'I am dreadfully bored; but have your own way, I'll bear it as long as I can!'

"Our conversations were generally of a most serious nature. On some occasions, he would advance French rationalism, and other views of the most atheistical kind, for no other reason than to make me combat them. It seemed impossible for him to see me, without being desirous of entering into an argument. A ball-room, where every eye was upon him, would have been as likely as any other place for him to have commenced the never-to-be-finished topic. I knew that he was a consistent Catholic, and revered the religion taught him by his mother; yet his education, and the influences of his many friends that were non-religionists, or at least steeped in Positivism, undoubtedly at times shook his faith. There was a religiousness in him (if I may so term it), that absolutely required communion with the Eternal Spirit to satisfy his nature.

"He had lofty imagination, sturdy logic, vivacious wit, tender sensibilities, strong passions, and an indomitable will; yet his purposes, plans, and wondrous energies were guided and harmonized by the spiritual element within him. Notwithstanding occasional outbreaks and yielding to temptations (for which due allowance must be made, he being human, and not divine), his faith in Christ, the image of the invisible God, never really swerved: therefore it seemed a positive pleasure to him to be vanquished by simple words of truth.

"When he was on the right side of a question, he was all-powerful. I remember meeting him at a quiet dinner-party: among the number was a gentleman, who, though Northern-born, took sides against the Union. This gentleman had annoyed me much by his proslavery views. He never hesitated to advance his most ultra opinions as to the right of the South to secede. We were seated next each other at the table. News had reached us from Port Royal that day. Gottschalk, without seeming to intend it, took the lead in the conversation, and expressed his views on the merits of the war, as also on slavery. I touched my neighbor, and said, 'Why don't you answer him? Now you have a fair opponent; you hear what he says.'

"He could not. Gottschalk seemed to have had a spirit of fire descend upon him. He spoke rapidly, brilliantly, with such power, such sweeping eloquence, such a crushing-out of pettiness, and upholding of the everlasting truth, that tears filled my eyes, — not mine alone, but all felt his power to uphold the right, and show us the good and true spirit which must prevail over wrong and selfishness.

"Gottschalk's memory was peculiar. I met him while travelling at Montreal. He joined our party at the theatre. With us was a young lady who saw a theatrical representation for the first time. He appeared delighted at the freshness of her remarks. Sometimes he helped her to understand the play in the most absurd manner. The play was 'School for Scandal.' I took him to task for something he said. Of course that started an argument. I told him I could not talk then, but after we returned to the hotel I would; and so I did. The greater part of the conversation was held while standing in the parlor; for it was getting late, and I had to join my friends: so we left off abruptly as the clock struck twelve. Our party left Montreal the next day without seeing him. Four months afterwards, we met in New York. He began the conversation exactly where we left off, not even premising it with, 'How do you do?' The moment his eyes rested on me, he was back again in imagination in the parlor at Montreal.

"He sometimes jokingly called me his brother, and said I thought too much for a sister in art. I do not think he admired, as a general thing, very intellectual women. He said their minds were illy balanced; and, to gain a great name in the world, they sacrificed all the most lovable and womanly qualities in attaining it. It was not likely I would agree to this, even if there was more truth than fiction in it; hence endless warfare on the subject whenever it was introduced.

"His power of concentration was great. He could abstract himself from every thing outside of what he wanted to do. In practising, he could keep his mind on the music at will. He was a great student and ardent admirer of Beethoven's music. I had the privilege, never to be forgotten, of hearing him play some of Beethoven's sonatas. He rarely played them in public; for he was so sentient, that pretenders stood no chance of deceiving him. He knew at a glance who enjoyed and comprehended the music; and he found the proportion so very small, that he did not bore the many for the pleasure of being cavilled at by the few. This is the usual recompense for the artist who plays classical music in general concerts.

"I had always supposed that Gottschalk was one of those natural players that do but comparatively little work; but I was greatly mistaken. I remember when he was studying 'Weber's Concert-Stück,' that he practised it hours at a time, although he seemed to play it perfectly well when he first played it. I remarked that I thought he knew it. 'Oh, no!' he replied: 'I find a new beauty every time I play it over. There is no end to study.'

"I said to him, one day, that I never used half the resources of my voice or art before the public, owing to nervousness, or, more properly, want of self-possession. 'To begin with, my heart beats so rapidly that it annoys me.'

"'Ah!' he replied, 'that is all owing to your neglect to make yourself at ease. The will is all-powerful to do this; you are no more nervous than I am, but you see *I never do commence* till I feel at ease. I make myself deliberate, and keep my head cool. I walk in very leisurely, I salute very moderately, I begin to take off my gloves as if I had come on for that purpose. Then I glance around in hopes of seeing an inspiring face, or at least a friendly one, so that my spirit may be in consonance with the music I am going to play, even if I am not in the mood.'

"'But I can't take off my gloves as you do.'

"'No,' he replied; 'but you can walk in deliberately, and speak to the accompanist. At any rate, never commence till you have mastered yourself.'

"True to this theory, on one occasion, when he accompanied me in a fugitive song of his own composition (from an opera lost, with many other valuable works, on a Southern railroad, the trunk never having been recovered), he turned to me, and spoke about the most indifferent subjects. He knew I was nervous; for he was late, and the place of the piece on the programme had to be changed on his account. He just quietly preluded the song,* speaking to me all the while till he thought I was at ease.

* This composition is in my possession. He had no copy of it himself, unless he has rewritten it since, which is not probable, as he recalled it especially for me. Gen. William Morris wrote the words for him.

"In regard to his playing, he stands alone in the perfection of phrasing, and exquisite shading of sentiment in the melody. In my estimation, many approach him in *technique*, but none in these points. He towers above all other pianists I have heard in this country or Europe, in giving voice and soul to the piano. He found an answering chord in this dry instrument that all other artists — I will not except one that I have heard — have yet to find. His melodies were pictures to the mind: one not only *heard*, but *saw* them. The familiar melody of 'Home, Sweet Home,' was absolutely sung on the piano by him: he formed, as it were, a *box-harmonicon* out of clanging wires.

"In his composition 'Last Hope,' we have a specimen of his religious temperament. I abstracted the melody from it and adapted the words, —

> 'My God, permit me not to be
> A stranger to myself and thee.'

I showed it to him, and underlined the words, —

> 'Amidst a thousand thoughts I rove,
> Forgetful of my highest love.'

The hymn was unknown to him. He read it, and seemed pleased to see his music wedded to such beautiful words. I told him it was one of our Sunday-evening hymns; so he would be sure to be thought of once a week, and that I should sing the words for him as well as myself.

"'Will you!' he said, and gave a never-to-be-forgotten glance. It expressed thanks and prayer.

"He always permitted me to scold him, if I thought he had done wrong; and on one occasion it was about something he explained away very readily. I was very glad, for I could not bear to see such a beautiful character marred by even a slight blemish. I said I was glad it was not true.

"'Promise me,' he said, 'you will never believe ill of me, unless it is impossible for you to do otherwise. So many lies are told about me, without any earthly foundation for them. I know you have set a high standard for me, and I wish to deserve and retain your esteem all my life.'

"I willingly gave him the promise. Thank God! I have had no reason to believe any of the thousand and one falsehoods, manufactured and set afloat by cupidity and malice, as a counterbalance for the great love and ever-ready friendship, that has ever been tendered to our lamented Gottschalk, by the refined and cultivated of every land which it was his pleasure to visit.

"His power to please was unlimited. He gained the friendship and love of men, young and old; and I have this day read a letter from one of his firmest and oldest friends. His words are, 'I shall never recover from this blow: I idolized him, — my whole plans of life are blank to me now.'

"Few men in the world have been so much loved; but, like all other high-strung spirits, he had to swallow bitter as well as sweet.

"He sometimes felt annoyed at the remarks made on account of his playing his own music so much in concerts. It would have been much more to the purpose to have blamed the listeners who enjoyed it.

"On one occasion, he had been solicited so strongly to play a favorite sonata of Beethoven's, at a small party of connoisseurs, that he acceded to the request. He began, and had not played more than ten measures, when one, who had been most anxious to hear it, began talking. Gottschalk went on, endeavoring to keep his mind so in the music as to gratify one fair girl who really enjoyed the sonata, and was familiar with it from beginning to end. At last, the buzz became general: then he gave vent to his pent-up annoyance, and went into the wildest *extempore* ever heard on a piano. He played on, he would not stop; but they did, wondering at him. At last, tired out, he flung himself into a chair, and received compliments of every kind for his rendering of the magnificent '*Beethoven sonata.*' It surpassed any thing they had ever heard. How his artist spirit suffered that night an artist only can know.

"Benevolence was a very marked feature in his character; and he was constantly besieged by those who knew his tenderness for suffering humanity. He was a Freemason, and liable to be called on at any time for aid, but never in vain. On one occasion, he was going to a suburb of a city for some purpose. When he arrived, the ferry-boat did not make trips in the evening. A poor laboring man came up just as Mr. Gottschalk was retracing his steps homeward. The man asked him if the boat had gone. To his reply 'Yes,' the poor man set up a lamentation. His family would be so anxious: he did not know what to do. Gottschalk said he would see what could be done. He found a man who had a row-boat. The trip was dangerous, but he would go over for twenty dollars. The poor man said he could not pay so much. 'Never mind, I will pay,' said Gottschalk. But the laborer refused to go at his cost. At last he said to the man, 'I want to go over; so jump in: it will cost no more to take you than for me to go alone.'

"His assertion prevailed; and the man jumped into the boat, and was soon with his family. There was a delicacy in his making the obligation light to the poor man, that was peculiarly his own.

"His feeling for cleanliness was so strong as to be thought by some 'over-fastidiousness.'

"He had a pupil who was in many respects an estimable man, but had to him most objectionable faults: his hands were hardly ever strictly clean, nails never; his teeth showed that tobacco was not a stranger to his mouth; his linen was often tumbled and soiled. Gottschalk meant to send him away after the first lesson. He made up his mind to this while he was pacing up and down the room, as was his habit when he gave a lesson; but when the man turned his beautiful eyes on him, and thanked him so heartily for his lesson, he had not the heart to tell him not to come. He endured it for three more lessons: no improvement had been made in his pupil's toilet. He asked Gottschalk something about his music: but he answered him, that the first thing necessary for a pianist and teacher was to be a gentleman; and the first thing necessary to being a gentleman was clean hands, well-kept nails and teeth, and unspotted linen. A man who was careless in these points lacked self-respect, and also respect for others.

"It was a strange sight to see the young man glance at his soiled cuffs and hands, and then jump up from the piano, and beg Gottschalk's pardon for thus offending. It corrected his carelessness, and pupil and master became firm friends.

"I have said but little about his compositions, for they are so well known. His larger works for orchestra it was not his fortune to have performed in New York.

"There are doubtless many who can give you much more testimony to his high-souled integrity and great worth than I can. C. M. B."

From a memorial sketch by Marguerite F. Aymar, the following extracts are gathered: —

"His mother was Mademoiselle Aimée de Braslé, a

granddaughter of the governor of Hayti of that name, under Louis XV.

"His early childhood was passed in a poetic and wild retirement, far from the noise of cities, or the realities of the world of men. On the romantic shores of Lake Pontchartrain he drew his first inspirations from the wisest and beneficent of all teachers, — Nature. At the age of four, he sought an outlet for his wonderful inspiration, for by no other name can it be called, on the piano; and not unfrequently at that tender, nay, baby age, his mother would be awakened in the long, still nights, by faint, sweet melodies from below, and descend to find the child fingering the 'beautiful cold keys,' with a marvellous rapt look on his little face. The first opera he ever heard, was 'Robert le Diable;' and, upon his return from the theatre, he sat down and played all the principal airs with a miraculous exactitude. Long years after, when the child had grown to a world-famous man, he says, speaking of the death of Meyerbeer, 'I will not attempt to tell you of my grief; to understand it, you must have been habituated, like myself, from infancy, to something little short of worship for this great genius, whose first *chef-d'œuvre*, "Robert le Diable," filled my early years with ineffable joy.'"

Of his sojourn in Switzerland she says, —

"When he concluded to take some necessary repose, he chose the wild, rare mountains of Switzerland, as in perfect consonance with his high-strung, vivid young nature. This season of rest, however, was not of long duration; but Gottschalk did not quit his retirement without leaving a lasting memorial of his goodness and generosity, so rarely met with in one so young, in the form of a hospital for the aged, which he founded at Yverclun."

Referring to his mountain life, she writes, —

"These years, especially one of them, passed in the grand solitude of the highest peak of the mountains of Guadaloupe, with no living soul near him save one faithful servant, Kaleb, Gottschalk affirms to have been the happiest of his life. There he gave himself up to mute illimitable communion with his God and nature. The pure, sweet air, the flowers and the birds, and the winds and the changeful clouds, were the food his spirit lived upon; and here he worked. Such work must have been his pleasure. 'Printemps d'Amour,' 'Jeunesse,' the 'Pastorella,' and many others, are dated from this dim, sweet year of loveliness. But again he was lured from his resting-place; and, after a series of glories in Havana, he once more returned to America, — New York."

. . . .

"Of Gottschalk's compositions, there is, or can be, but one opinion regarding them as a whole, — wonderful in their elastic, vivid refinement of culture and sensibility, their subtle, voluptuous charm of rhythm, and melodic significance, and in their marvellous suggestive qualities. There was ever a faint, sweet *something* left to each listener when Gottschalk had finished playing one of his own compositions, — a delicious, untold emanation, which each could interpret to his own fancy.

"But there are those among his works which evince the grand, free soul, soaring above the earth and its earthly passions, into that heaven of divine inspiration. 'Jerusalem,' for instance, is mighty in its solemn grandeur; and its under-tone is the mysterious passion of the soul, not the luxurious modulations of the heart. The symphony of the 'Siege of Saragossa' is another exhibit of the splendor of musical phraseology as an interpretation of the higher emotions, untouched by the softer moods he so usually fell into. And again, 'La Nuit des Tropiques,' one of the most exquisitely thrilling, high-wrought, and pure symphonies we ever listened to. Gottschalk's was a great soul, and his inspiration was from the Giver of all great and good gifts. Not always did the soul rise above its poetic, sensuous, human accompaniments; but that it did sometimes is undeniable.

"Of his private life, we have no word to say, save the pure, good truth. He was a devoted son, and, at the time of his death, was looking forward to the fulfilment of a last request of his mother's, — a pilgrimage to the Holy Land. A more than devoted brother; and lasting monuments of his large-hearted charities are not failing in any land where his name and face have been known. A true American, proud of his birthright, and an ardent lover of liberty, one of the fairest jewels in his crown was the liberation of his slaves in Louisiana. His triumphs, from every point of view, were unprecedented in the annals of pianists, — the recipient of medals and orders from nearly every crowned head in Europe and South America. His personal friends were many and warm; and in numberless households the news of his death, rendered doubly hard in that it occurred in a foreign land, will cause no ordinary grief.

"To his enemies, — for, like every great man, he had them, — we can but say, he is dead, — gone from your sight into the great hereafter, whither God hath called him. To his friends: his memory, and the undying consolation of his works, will speak in a voice well beloved, since they are a part of himself."

Here is another, from the pen of Mr. George Upton. It is too truthfully beautiful to be omitted: —

IN MEMORIAM.

"And poor Louis Gottschalk is dead!

"From the heart of the tropics, which he loved so well, — for his whole nature was tropical, — into the heart of this northern winter comes the sad news borne on southern gales, — Louis Gottschalk is dead.

"And when the recording angel saw him coming, and called out, 'Louis Moreau Gottschalk,' how quickly he must have answered, with that sad smile kindling on his face, 'Died on the field of duty.'

"It seems but yesterday, although it was a cold winter afternoon in 1864, that I bade him good-by, little dreaming that it was for the last time. I had been sitting with him all that afternoon; and he had played to me, in his dreamy way, the 'Midsummer-Night's Dream' and some of Mendelssohn's 'Lieder ohne Worte' as I had never heard them before, — as I may never hear them again. Hour after hour he played, only pausing to light a fresh cigar, saying nothing, but weaving into a gorgeous web of music the thoughts of the great masters.

"And some small souls, who could only see the outer man, had told me he was affected and egotistic. Affected and egotistic! This man, who lived in music; whose dreams were embroidered with threads of melody; who was as delicate in his tastes as a refined woman; whose soul shut up like a flower from contact with strangers, and only opened and expanded to receive a friend!

"The history of his life is told in a few words. He was born in New Orleans, in 1829. His mother was a French Creole, and his father a Spanish Jew; and such a love as he gave to that father and mother is rare in this world. Like all musical geniuses, he lisped in music, and gave unmistakable evidences of his talent at a very early age. He went to Paris when he was only twelve years of age, and, after studying music four years, came back to this country, and made his first public appearance as a pianist in 1845. From that time until 1853, he made a professional tour of Europe. In 1853, he returned to this country, and up to his death had divided his time between the United States and South America. That is the sum of his life, as far as mere incidents are concerned; but it was only a small part.

"I think that our country has never been blessed with such a real musical genius as Louis Gottschalk. He was thoroughly original. His music was unlike any other. Nearly all pianists are plagiarists. Gottschalk was original, because he wrote out of his inner nature. Run over his compositions, — the 'Printemps D'Amour,' 'Murmures Eoliens,' 'La Colombe,' the 'Banjo Fantasia,' that inimitable 'Berceuse,' the 'Chant du Soldat,' the 'Last Hope,' the 'Marche de Nuit,' the 'Ojos Creollos,' the 'Souvenirs D'Andalousie,' his ballad 'Serenade,' the 'O ma Charmante Caprice,' and his splendid instrumentation of the overture to 'William Tell,' or the little gems of waltzes and polkas which he published under the familar *nom de plume* of 'Seven Octaves,' — and see if you can find their motives anywhere else in the whole realm of music. He was as distinctive as Chopin, and as dreamy and suggestive as Robert Franz. And what a *technique* he had! His runs were like the rippling of water, his octaves as clear and distinct as the flash of a diamond, and his touch purity itself. Under the magic of his long, delicate fingers, a piano sung like a rich soprano.

"He was thoroughly tropical in his nature, — dreamy, abstracted, and warm-blooded. A superficial observer would have called him indolent, for he passed much time in reveries; and many of these reveries, in his inspired moments, he interpreted upon the piano, which have never seen paper. He was as uneasy in these cold climes as some rare-plumaged bird pining in its gilded cage. It was only among these fiery birds, among the rank, luxurious vegetation, among the dark-eyed Spanish beauties of the tropics, that he really lived. His best compositions were born in the warm breath of southern climes; and all that he wrote in the temperate zones were but reminiscences of, and yearnings for, that country. He was faultlessly delicate in his tastes, and could never sympathize with any thing that was grotesque, bizarre, or rude. His physical organization was moulded of the finest clay. His hands were a study of beauty. His voice was low and musical, and his face the very embodiment of tropical beauty. Once your friend, he was always your friend; for he loved with intensity, and hated with ardor. He made but few friends: perhaps would have made more if there had been more who could understand and appreciate such a nature as his, which had so little in common with other men. And under all this warmth and delicacy of nature flowed an undercurrent of sadness, which pervaded his whole being, and tinged all his music. It was a sadness not dependent upon circumstances, nor growing out of any fate, but a part of himself, and always a component part of all true artists. It was not so dark nor so turbid a torrent as that which wrecked Chopin, not such a deep regret as that which separated Beethoven from men, and made him stand out like some solitary mountain, looming up in awful grandeur; but rather a tender feeling of regret, 'the tender grace of a day that is dead.' It was broad enough and deep enough to give character to his life and color to his music.

"He died as any musician would like to die, I should think, in the midst of his friends, standing before his orchestra with his baton in his hands, and, by a sad coincidence, directing one of his own compositions, 'La Morte.' It was Mozart and his Requiem over again.

"And the singers closed their books, and the instruments ceased, and in place of their sound came the terrible, solemn silence of death. And on the next day the same singers and players tenderly bore him to the populous Acre of God. And men and women whom he had charmed and made better with the great blessing of his music came each to drop into the open grave some flower of grateful love and remembrance. And royalty deemed it an honor to touch the pall of the dead musician. So, under those blue skies, and amid the fiery-plumaged birds and gorgeous-petalled flowers he loved so well, they laid him down to sleep his long, last sleep. And from this desk, under these cold, gray skies, in which no bird sings, and from these frozen plains, upon which no flower blooms, do I send to-day, down to that Southern grave, this slight tribute of admiration I am glad to own, of friendship it was my good fortune to share.

"And as I thus say good-night to the dead friend and musician, I am reminded of those lines of Gerald Massey's: —

> 'The dear ones who are worthiest of our love
> Below are also worthiest above.
> Too lofty is his place in glory now
> For hands like ours to reach and wreathe his brow:
> A few pale flowers we plant upon his tomb,
> Watered with tears to make them breathe and bloom.'"

From "The World" (New York) of Jan. 23, I am glad to copy this appreciative sketch, written before he left the United States for South America. It is a most fitting tribute to place upon his tomb: —

"With the roar of cannon and tramp of armed men resounding through the land, and the fair young face of the Republic disfigured to our eyes by the deep furrows of war, it is pleasant to know, that, in certain nooks and corners, gentler sounds of harmony still linger, and that ateliers exist where men's fancies grow on canvas from day to day into soothing visions of loveliness. The scarlet and gold and general paraphernalia of war are too tempting to pallet and brush, not to be seized on with avidity, and reproduced with marvellous truth; but it is more agreeable to pass over accurate representations of the Irish Zouaves, with Celtic features, not purely classical in outlines, glowing defiantly under the red cap of the Arab, and Teutonic cavalrymen clinging clumsily to their steeds, and turn for solace to the grand, solemn shores of Niagara, to wander amid the tangled luxuriance of the Heart of the Andes, or to bask in the sweet silence of twilight in the wilderness. There are icebergs, too, floating in the Arctic Sea, frozen white and mute with horror at the dread secrets of ages; but, responsive to the versatile talent of the hand that creates them, they glow with prismatic light of many colors. Mr. Church irradiates the frozen regions with the coruscations of his own genius, bringing to these lonely, despairing masses of ice the revivifying hope and promise of warmer climates. In pondering over the sad mystery of these icebergs, we float down again to tropical seas and islands; and, as we linger under the shade of palm and banana tree, the rude chant of the negro strikes the ear in the grotesque and characteristic framework of the 'Bananier,' the plaintive melody of 'La Savane' sighs past on the evening breeze, Spanish eyes flash out temptingly from the enticing cadence of the 'Ojos Criollos,' and Spanish guitars tinkle in the soft moonlight of the 'Minuit a Seville,' and tropical life awakes to melody under the touch of the Creole poet of the piano, Mr. Gottschalk. There are many beings, otherwise estimable, to whom the tropical sense is wanting; who are ever suspicious of malaria lurking under the rich, glossy leaves of the orange groves; who look with disgust and loathing at the exaggerated proportions and venomous nature of all creeping things; who find the succulence of the fruit unpleasant to the taste, and the flowers, though fair to the eye, deadly as the upas-tree to all other sense; for whom it is no compensation to feel, with the first breath of morning air, the dull, leaden weight of life lifted, or no happiness to watch the sea heaving and palpitating with delight under the rays of the noonday sun, and to know that the stars at night droop down lovingly and confidingly to the embrace of warm tropical earth. With an insensibility to these influences, there can be but little sympathy or appreciation of the works of Mr. Gottschalk; for all that is born of the tropics partakes of its beauties and its defects, its passionate languor, its useless profusion, and its poetic tenderness. And where else in the United States can we look for a spontaneous gush of melody? Plymouth Rock and its surroundings have not hitherto seemed favorable to the growth and manifestations of musical genius; for the old Puritan element, in its savage intent to annihilate the æsthetic part of man's nature, under the deadening dominion of its own blue-laws, and to crush out whatever of noble inspiration had been vouchsafed to man by his Creator, rarely sought relief in outbursts of song. Psalmody appears to have been the chief source of musical indulgence; and for many a long, weary year hymns of praise, nasal in tone and dismal in tendency, have ascended from our prim forefathers to the Throne of Grace on high. Such depressing musical antecedents have not prepared New England for greater efforts of melody than are to be found in the simple ballads supposed to originate with the plantation negro, who, in addition to his other burdens, is thus chosen to assume the onerous one of Northern song, as being the only creature frivolous enough to indulge in vain carolling. If we can scarcely affirm that the Americans are yet a musical people, that they would be is an undeniable fact, and one constantly evinced in their lavish support of artists, from the highest to the lowest grade. Among the musical aspirants to popular favor, none has of late enjoyed so large a share of notice and admiration as Mr. Gottschalk; and, to return from our recent digression, we will proceed to the consideration of his compositions. Fragmentary and suggestive as are his ideas, there is infinite method and system in their treatment. Avoiding thus far what is termed *sustained effort*, and which frequently implies the same demands on the patience of the listener as on the creative power of the composer, Mr. Gottschalk's compositions contain just so much of the true poetic vein as can be successfully digested and enjoyed in a piano piece of moderate length. With the power to conceive, and the will and discipline of mind to execute, there is no reason why, with perhaps a diminished tendency to fritter away positive excellence at the shrine of effect, enduring proofs of the genius of our American pianist should not be given to the world. As a mere player, the popularity of Mr. Gottschalk with the uninitiated masses is due, in a great measure, to his tact in discerning the American craving for novelty and sensation, and to his native originality and brilliancy, which allow him to respond so fully to these exigencies of public taste, as to possess on all occasions the key-note to applause. The faculty of never degenerating into dulness, the rock on which most pianists are wrecked in early youth, is another just cause for insuring to our compatriot the pre-eminence which he enjoys. Viewed from a critical point, the mechanical endowments and acquirements of Gottschalk are such as to enable him to subject his playing to the test of keenest analysis without detriment to his reputation. For clearness and limpidity of touch and unerring precision, for impetuosity of style combined with dreamy delicacy, he has few rivals. The evenness and brilliancy of his trill are unequalled; the mechanical process required to produce it being lost to sight in the wonderful birdlike nature of the effect. In the playing of classical music, Mr. Gottschalk has to contend against his own individuality. This individuality, naturally intense, and of a kind calculated to meet with public favor, has been cultivated and indulged in to such an extent, as to prove an occasional obstacle to the exclusive absorption and utter identification with the ideas of another composer that classical music demands. In the mere matter of execution, there is no difficulty which the fingers of this skilful pianist cannot overcome; and his intellectual grasp of a subject enables him to discern and interpret the beauties of all musical themes: but where an earnest, passionate interest in the music of the old masters is not felt by the performer, it is rarely communicated to his hearers. The world of letters, however, has not seemingly regretted the inability of Byron to trammel his muse with the uncongenial fetters of Pope's metre, and has certainly never quarrelled with Tom Moore for not assuming the manners and diction of the revered Samuel Johnson, LL.D. With due allowance for difference of latitude, and wide difference of aim and pursuit, the contemplation of the master of Creole melody recalls to us a genius which found utterance in song, none the less melodious that it was written, not sung. The 'ashen sky,' and 'crisped, sear leaves of the lonesome October,' so thrillingly pictured by Edgar Poe in his 'Ulalume,' find echo in the foreboding sadness of the opening bars to Gottschalk's 'Last Hope;' and as both poems grow in vague, dreamy sound, they culminate in a cry of smothered despair at the tomb where all hopes lie buried with the lost Ulalume. The same weird conception and eccentricity of design, with knowledge of rhythmical effect and extreme carefulness of finish, are prominent traits of both artists; and the American disregard of tradition, as evinced in all enterprises, whether literary, artistic, or commercial, and which readily infects the simple sojourner among us as well as the happy being born to republican privileges, marks alike the nationality of poet and pianist."

"The London Orchestra" says, —

"We have had already occasion to say that Gottschalk was not only a pianist and eminent composer, but a writer remarkable for the variety and freshness of his thoughts as well as for his rare and profound instruction; and his premature death is no less a loss for music than it is for literature.

"His morality excelled his intellectual manhood. Charitable, good, kind, free from ridiculous vanity, capable of the greatest abnegation for his friends, and even for those who were indifferent to him, he combined those rare qualities which made him the idol of all those who had the happiness of knowing him. A model of the noblest and most delicate address, the musical art was to him an adoration, — a holy thing. He was not only a man of talent, but a man of genius. His compositions bear the seal of perfect individuality.

"The news of his death will surprise painfully and afflict the musical world; but the tomb which covers his remains will not conceal from the face of the earth the name which time cannot erase."

A Rio Janeiro journal, speaking of the death of Gottschalk, says, —

"His music has ceased for us on earth, but the memory of those exalted strains can never die. No other hand can gather in such harmonies, no other mind weave melodies so entrancing to the soul. The land that gave him birth may well be proud, for now no niche in its temple of fame is unfilled. Poets, painters, statesmen has she crowned with immortelles, and now a musician, American born and nurtured, wins the brightest laurels of undying renown."

Another Rio journal adds, —

"The mass of the 30th day for Gottschalk took place to-day in the church of San Francisco de Paula, under the auspices of the Philharmonic Society of this city. The attendance was very large; and the ceremonies were conducted with a degree of pomp and splendor rarely witnessed on similar occasions. It will be long before the memory of this great artist will pass away. Scarcely a day comes without some new tribute to his worth in the shape of a musical or poetical composition; and, in the shop-windows everywhere, one continually meets his photograph, — a noble head, with handsome, well-cut features, marking the possession not only of rare intelligence, but also of a kind and generous heart."

And last, there comes from one of whom Gottschalk once said to me, "Warren's sympathy for me is perfect: he understands every phase of my nature" : —

To Madame Octavia Hensel, Boston.

6, Garden Street, Brooklyn, April 20, 1870.

Dear Madame, — What can I give you but a hurried sketch of my long friendship with the dear departed.

Gottschalk came to Albany (where I was then living) in October, 1855. I then heard him for the first time, and succumbed at once. It was love at first sight, — love for the man, his genius, his most extraordinary playing, and the utter (inner) simplicity of character, which I discovered at a glance; although many, who were never willing to do him justice, saw only the outside man in evening dress, decorated with medals, and doing his utmost to please a promiscuous audience. They knew not Gottschalk in private life, at the piano (he was always there), with a few warm friends listening, — the tender-hearted, sensitive artist and loyal friend, ready with extended hand to help any poor struggling wight of the key-board, — ready with a good word and resistless smile to reward the efforts of his *confrères* of the profession.

I could go on in this strain at great length, and give you many touching evidences of his goodness and largeness of heart; for we were together often and often, and under all kinds of circumstances.

In 1860, I moved to my present home; and soon after he returned from South America, and for a few years I was more intimate with him than ever before. He had wonderful power to move those around him. He was musical electricity itself. I could mention many instances, but will only allow myself one incident. He was just beginning to be very serious; and he was a most intense observer, and with strong sympathies on the right side of the question. I shall never forget a scene at the house of Mr. Wm. T. Blodgett of New York. It was a most distinguished gathering of artistic and celebrated gentlemen, from everywhere and of all kinds. Church's picture, "The Heart of the Andes," was then the *lion* in a collection of pictures as rare as their owner is liberal and beloved as a patron of fine arts; and the painter himself was of the group, of which Gottschalk was another; and happy is he who can remember to have been present that evening. There was much admiring to be done by eyesight, and much talking that had responsive and delighted listening,; but the ear needed its *sweetest* refreshment as well as the eye and palate, and some music was a necessity. Gottschalk, as usual, was amiable, and most happy to entertain his distinguished audience. He played as an artist never can at a concert; and his listeners were correspondingly appreciative, — all except one Englishman (maybe a duke) who made some slur on all that was American in music, which brought Gottschalk to his feet in defence of his brother-workers. White as a sheet, and in his excited and overwhelming eloquence, he told them of a melody then being sung by regiment after regiment, marching down Broadway *en route* for the cars to Washington; of a melody they learned at home in the far West, and that they would carry with them, and sing it on the battle-field; of a melody that would sustain them in the thickest fight. And, on the spur of the moment, he sprang to the piano again, and gave such an astounding rhapsody on George F. Root's well-known "We'll Rally Round the Flag," as is entirely beyond description. I never heard any thing like it, and never will again; for Liszt himself could not have appreciated the situation, and Liszt is not Creole-American. The effect was earthquakean almost. These men of art are enthusiastic; and they were frantic. The uproar could have been heard a mile. Gottschalk was nearly killed with embraces, — and the gentleman from England had departed.

I have been with my dear friend, time after time, when

he has carried his listeners beyond space, and affected them with a magician's power. His playing was often most solemn and religious, when the hammer could not be heard against the string, and the whole thing was organ-toned. His use of the pedals was a study, producing results the most unique and interesting. But what is the use of reviewing what we all know of his playing. It united every thing, — power the most magnificent, dexterity unequalled. Think of the trill and cadenza in "*Murmures Éoliens*", — delicacy and grace beyond criticism, and a largeness and breadth peculiar to the man; and, lastly, the Gottschalk originality, — a something unlike any thing or anybody else. And how sad to me — so sad, that, were I a woman, the tears would flow afresh — to know that on this earth we shall never hear his like again!

In public, our dear friend was the expounder of his own school of composition; for which he has been taxed heavily by all those who do not believe in the works of living composers, and some others too. Now that he is really dead (and it seems impossible), we may expect some justice by and by; and who knows but in the course of a few hundred years the name of Gottschalk may be just a little classical (What is classical? — conundrum to be given up)?

At a concert which I had the pleasure of arranging for him and Madame De la Grange, at Albany, in May, 1856, he played, —

Impromptu in A flat	*Chopin.*
"If I were a Bird,"—Etude . . .	*Henselt.*
Benevenuti Cellini of Berlioz, transcribed by	*Liszt.*
Silver Spring	*Wm. Mason.*
Fantasie "Lucia"	*Gottschalk.*
Last Hope	"
Marche de Nuit	"
Banjo	"

I have yet to hear Chopin's Impromptu rendered with any such fire and intense feeling as on that occasion. His nature sprang out to meet the idiosyncrasy of Chopin's works; and I am happy in knowing that I have heard our friend interpret (in private if not in public) the majority of the works of the wonderful pianoforte poet. Yes: and I know of the sincere worship that Gottschalk laid at the feet of *that* master, and also of his reverence and study of the greatest of masters, the immortal Beethoven.

Gottschalk felt that while he lived he must demonstrate the genius of Gottschalk; and where is there a musician of any like talent who would not do just the same thing?

Our friend was faithful to *his* friends unto death. The touching letter from his sister, which you kindly sent me to read, is ample proof; and I trust you will publish it.

To the Chickerings he was a tower of strength: for, although tempting offers were made him to leave that house and use other pianos, he could not change his opinion or do a mean thing; and where he had in the first place given that honest opinion, there he abided. No pianos suited his finger so well. Their power and brilliancy added to his triumphs; their great durability on his long tours over the country made him grateful; and he is entirely identified with the house of Chickering. So with all his friends: he never forgot them. He was 'way above the small envyings and jealousies of the profession. He wished all well, and was lovable to the last degree. Sympathetic and clinging, he appealed to the tender affection of those he loved best continually.

His last picture, sent to me from Rio last summer, is before me as I finish this hasty tribute to his memory. I look at the dear face which often looked at mine in life (you know his way) while the fingers rolled forth the harmonies. Would

that I had been able to say something more worthy the ever-to-be-lamented subject of your book!
Sincerely your friend,
GEORGE WILLIAM WARREN.

And thus I close my simple sketches of one whose noble and beautiful life should indeed be an example to those who still labor here for the advancement of music, the only science we are assured we shall find in the heaven-realm of God!

Words cannot fully express the meaning or the mission of music upon earth; but power is sometimes given a human soul to impart, through wondrous combination of tones, pictures to the imagination, until a spiritual gleam of knowledge is through sympathy vouchsafed to others, of the subtle power of music for the good of human kind. If those who hold this key to the glorious realm of purest love and passionate longing for an unattained bliss are but true to themselves, and use aright their God-given power, life will be rich in splendor of intellectual enjoyment; and when shadows of death encompass them, when the tidal waves of the dark river chill the life-blood of the heart, their spirits shall rise, in the rapture of chanting seraphim, far above the stars' triumphal symphony, borne on the breath of heavenly anthems, through gates of gleaming pearl and flashing jasper-stone, forever onward to that Holy of Holies, where the voice of God thrills the majestic harmonies of angel and archangel with the simple tone-power of the words, —

"Well done, thou good and faithful servant! thou hast been faithful over a few things; I will make thee ruler over many things: enter thou into the joy of thy Lord."

DITSON & CO'S PUBLICATIONS.

Beethoven's Letters, 1790-1826. From
the collection of Dr. L. Nohl. Translated by Lady Wallace. With a portrait and facsimile. 1 vol., Cloth. $2.00.

In this collection of his private correspondence we have an interior view of the great composer—showing us what he was, what he did, what he suffered, and what was the point of view from which ne surveyed art and life. Beethoven, in music, is quite as great a name as Milton's in poetry; and among the thousands who have been charmed, thrilled and exalted by his wonderful melodies, and who really appreciate the originality, creativeness and might of his genius, these letters cannot fail to find delighted readers.—*Boston Transcript.*

Mozart's Letters, 1769-1791. Translated,
from the collection of L. Nohl, by Lady Wallace. 2 vols., Cloth. With a portrait and facsimile. $1.75. each vol.

These letters have the charm of Mozart's loving melodies. They are not less gay and tender, not less tremulous with sensibility, and seem to let us into the secret of his felicitous ease in composition—the secret of a bird "Singing of summer with full-throated Ease.—*G. H. Lewes, in Fortnightly Review.*

Life of Rossini. By H. SUTHERLAND
EDWARDS, with a portrait by GUSTAVE DORE. Price $1.57.

"An eminently interesting, readable, and trustworthy book. Mr. Edwards was instinctively looked to for a life of Rossini, and the result is a very satisfactory one. The salient features of Rossini's life and labors are grouped in admirable order; and the book, while it conveys every thing necessary to an accurate idea of its subject, is as interesting as a novel."—*London Sunday Times.*

"Mr. Edwards has rendered a service to his brother connoisseurs and critics, and not less to the general public, in these lively and attractive pages. The work must be acknowledged a very fit memorial of Rossini. It is the fruit of great knowledge, and much critical aptitude."—*London Star.*

"Mr. Edwards's 'Life of Rossini' is eminently readable and interesting. We have seldom read a book about a great man so attractively written."—*London Orchestra.*

Mozart. A Romantic Biography.
From the German of HERIBERT RAU, by EDWARD ROWLAND SILL. Cloth, $1.00.

"A story full of insight and artistic sympathy,—a beautiful memorial and tribute to the life, the trials, the triumphs, and the memory of genius; and, besides all this, has the charm of a fascinating narrative, and the value of a genuine memoir."—*Boston Transcript.*

DITSON & CO'S PUBLICATIONS.

Life of Chopin. By F. Liszt. Translated from the French by MRS. MARTHA WALKER COOK. 1 vol. Cloth. Price, $1.50.

"In spite of the trammels of words, it gives expression to the same subtle and ethereal conceptions which inspired the genius of Liszt as a musical artist. As a sketch of the life of the great composer, it possesses an interest with which few biographical works can compare; but no details of incident could imprison the soul of the author, and a fine æsthetic aroma breathes from every page, fragrant with the blossoming out of a rich original nature, as well as with an exquisite sense of art."—*Tribune.*

"The American art-world may congratulate itself on the possession of such a work, and students and lovers of the great Chopin will thank the translator and Mr. Leypoldt for such a gift. It will lie on every music-stand with the beautiful thin volumes of Chopin music."—*Dwight's Journal of Music.*

"We wish the book would be bought by every amateur, because it does not only give an insight into one of the most peculiar geniuses of modern times and into his music, but it also shows us, more than perhaps any thing else, the high imaginative powers of Liszt, the poet, composer, and pianist."—*Musical Review.*

Musical Sketches. By ELISE POLKO. Translated from the Sixth German Edition by FANNY FULLER. 1 vol. Cloth. Price, $1.75.

"The style of the articles is rich, eloquent, and impressive. The author is a musical enthusiast, and these productions are thoroughly inspired with the enthusiasm. The sketch of Bach and his performance of 'A mighty fortress is our God,' before the Court at Dresden, contains some passages displaying a luxuriousness of description scarcely surpassed by De Quincey in his happiest moods. No lover or student of music, who has a soul for its beauties, can fail to enjoy these graceful memorials of its triumphs and marvels, and these pictured joys and aspirations of its mighty teachers."—*Publishers' Circular.*

"A charming little book, containing gems from the pen of one of the most felicitous of writers. Sweetly, simply, and at times pathetically, are the dreams and experiences of artists such as Bach, Gluck, Handel, Haydn, and others of equal note, described and wondered over."—*Home Journal.*

Mendelssohn's Letters.

With a Catalogue of all his musical compositions. Translated from the German by LADY WALLACE. 2 vols. Cloth. Price $1.75 per vol.

"There is not a page, in this delightful volume, which would not yield matter of pleasure and instruction to the reader. There is no leaving this book, which is fuller of artistic precepts and record of practice, and personal indications of character, than any collection of musical letters which, till now, has seen daylight. There will be no end of appeal to it, so long as people shall live who believe that Music is no sensual enchantress, no enervating Dalilah, but a Muse, a Grace, a power, a truth, and a humanizing influence among the arts."—*London Athenæum.*

"We wish our religious societies would call out a few of the letters of this man and scatter them broadcast over the land: they would indeed be 'leaves for the healing of the nations.'"—*Atlantic Monthly.*

Life of Felix Mendelssohn Bartholdy.

From the German of W. A. LAMPADIUS, with Supplementary Sketches by JULIUS BENEDICT, HENRY F. CHORLEY, LUDWIG RELLSTAB, BAYARD TAYLOR, R. S. WILLIS, and J. S. DWIGHT. Edited and translated by WILLIAM LEONHARD GAGE. With portrait. 1 vol., Cloth. Price, $1.75.

"The short but interesting life by Lampadius, is still the best, the only life of real value....... With the letters for illustration, it will be impossible for any musical person to read it without interest."—*Dwight's Journal of Music.*

"The American editor has well earned the thanks of the public by the assiduity with which he has sought for available materials, and the taste and skill with which he has applied them to the illustration of his interesting theme."—*New York Tribune.*

"It is a pleasant, cheerful book, this 'Life.' It seems to have been a labor of love to the translator, and while it tells much that is interesting about the composer, it is also to be admired for its entertaining character, in a literary view."—*Home Journal.*

www.ingramcontent.com/pod-product-compliance
Lightning Source LLC
Chambersburg PA
CBHW020833230426
43666CB00007B/1205